David L. Edgell Sr., PhD

Managing Sustainable Tourism
A Legacy for the Future

"**D**r. Edgell is ideally suited to author a text of this nature—a scholar, consultant, public policymaker, business operator, and experienced traveler, he truly understands the challenges and opportunities of sustainable tourism.

This publication provides a straightforward and insightful view of the interfacing of sustainability and tourism. Policymakers at all levels, business owners and operators, planners, and travelers interested in acting in a more responsible manner will all find information useful to improve their ability to implement sustainable tourism practices.

Edgell's work accurately and effectively documents the evolution of sustainable tourism thinking and the actions necessary to ensure that tourism ultimately fulfills its role as a powerful force for global action. He has captured the essence of the triple bottom line of sustainable tourism—the environmental, sociocultural, and economic arguments for embracing sustainable behaviors by the many and varied sectors of the world's largest industry."

Patrick T. Long, EdD
Professor, Leeds School of Business
and Faculty Director,
Center for Sustainable Tourism,
University of Colorado at Boulder;
President Elect,
American Leisure Academy

"**T**his comprehensive book on sustainable tourism should be required reading for everyone interested in tourism. The author is masterful in defining strategies and using case studies to explain best practices in generating long-term economic return on tourism investment."

Kurtis M. Ruf, PDM, BS
Partner, Ruf Strategic Solutions;
Author, *Contemporary Database Marketing*

More pre-publication
REVIEWS, COMMENTARIES, EVALUATIONS . . .

"**W**ith many of the world's unique sites coming under increasing demographic and environmental pressures, this book is a most welcome addition to the emerging field of sustainable tourism. The world's leading authority guides the reader step-by-step through the complex issues and challenging choices facing tourist destinations. The case studies of successful tourism developments provide concrete examples of how local areas can bring all stakeholders together to come up with creative solutions that generate income for the local population, preserve the environment for future generations, enhance cultural heritage, and provide visitors with a meaningful experience. This book marks the beginning of an important paradigm shift from consumer tourism to travel with a purpose. It is highly recommended for professionals already active in tourism development and management as well as students contemplating a career in the field.

There is something for everyone in this book: environmentalists will appreciate the sensitivity to protecting and enhancing nature; rural development specialists and regional planners will benefit from advice on planning, marketing, and community involvement; and cultural preservationists will find ample material and important information on protecting and enhancing heritage sites. This book will become the reference standard for future discussions on sustainable tourism."

Thoric Cederstrom, PhD
Vice President,
Counterpart International

"**D**r. Edgell has done it again: written a new must-read book for anyone in the world's largest business—tourism. His use of diverse case studies in sustainable tourism, where he has hands-on experience, makes each chapter come alive.

This work is a rare combination of theory, practical application, and Dr. Edgell's willingness to take some risks by looking into the future and making predictions about sustainable tourism. He combines a good dose of 'how-to' with an equally important shot of 'how-NOT-to.'"

Frederick M. Bush, MA
Associate Director for Development and Constituent Relations,
Development Office, Woodrow Wilson International Center for Scholars

THHP

The Haworth Hospitality Press®
An Imprint of The Haworth Press, Inc.
New York • London • Oxford

Managing Sustainable Tourism
A Legacy for the Future

Managing Sustainable Tourism
A Legacy for the Future

David L. Edgell Sr., PhD

The Haworth Hospitality Press®
An imprint of The Haworth Press, Inc.
New York • London • Oxford

For more information on this book or to order, visit
http://www.haworthpress.com/store/product.asp?sku=5489

or call 1-800-HAWORTH (800-429-6784) in the United States and Canada
or (607) 722-5857 outside the United States and Canada

or contact orders@HaworthPress.com

Published by

The Haworth Hospitality Press®, an imprint of The Haworth Press, Inc., 10 Alice Street, Binghamton, NY 13904-1580.

PUBLISHER'S NOTE
The development, preparation, and publication of this work has been undertaken with great care. However, the Publisher, employees, editors, and agents of The Haworth Press are not responsible for any errors contained herein or for consequences that may ensue from use of materials or information contained in this work. The Haworth Press is committed to the dissemination of ideas and information according to the highest standards of intellectual freedom and the free exchange of ideas. Statements made and opinions expressed in this publication do not necessarily reflect the views of the Publisher, Directors, management, or staff of The Haworth Press, Inc., or an endorsement by them.

Cover design by Lora Wiggins.

Library of Congress Cataloging-in-Publication Data

Edgell, David L.
    Managing sustainable tourism : a legacy for the future / David L. Edgell, Sr.
      p. cm.
    Includes bibliographical references and index.
    ISBN-13: 978-0-7890-2770-2 (hc. : alk. paper)
    ISBN-10: 0-7890-2770-4 (hc. : alk. paper)
    ISBN-13: 978-0-7890-2771-9 (pbk. : alk. paper)
    ISBN-10: 0-7890-2771-2 (pbk. : alk. paper)
1. Ecotourism—Management. 2. Heritage tourism—Management. I. Title.

G156.5.E26E38 2006
338.4'791'068—dc22

2005010627

To my late parents,
Edna Mae and John J. Edgell Sr. who were always there for me
and
FOR THE NEXT GENERATION
that includes
The children of David L. Edgell Sr.
David
Nelson
Rodney
Daughter-in-law
Silvia
Grandchildren
Amanda and Lucca

We have not inherited the Earth from our ancestors.
We have only borrowed it from our children.

Ancient proverb

with a special dedication to
Sarah J. Gust
the calm, patient, supportive wife who puts up with me

ABOUT THE AUTHOR

David L. Edgell Sr., PhD, is a tenured professor and the Director of the Institute for Tourism at East Carolina University in Greenville, North Carolina. He is an author, speaker, and consultant, having written over six books and over 100 articles on tourism, trade, and economic development, and having made several presentations here and abroad. Dr. Edgell was one of the architects of the National Tourism Policy Act of 1981, which established the United States Travel and Tourism Administration, the National Tourism Policy Council, and the United States Travel and Tourism Advisory Board. For several years he led efforts in the government to increase international tourism to the United States including serving in the highest post as Under Secretary of Commerce for Travel and Tourism. He is the only person to ever receive all three of the department's highest medal awards for his leadership in trade, tourism, and economic development. He also served at one point in his career as the Commissioner of Tourism for the U.S. Virgin Islands, Vice President for Strategic Marketing at MMG Worldwide (a marketing firm that only services clients in tourism, travel, and hospitality), and Adjunct Professor of Tourism at George Washington University and at the University of Hawaii.

CONTENTS

Foreword

Worldwide tourism has grown enormously since the beginning of the twenty-first century, and it will likely continue to do so over the next several years if the international tourism community fully recognizes, endorses, and promotes the concepts of sustainable tourism.

Sustainable tourism is a part of an overall shift that recognizes that orderly economic growth, combined with concerns for the environment and quality-of-life social values, will be the driving force for long-term progress in tourism development and policies. *Managing Sustainable Tourism: A Legacy for the Future* presents some policy prescriptions for orderly growth and development that adhere to an important set of criteria for improving the quality of life through sustainable tourism.

The opportunity that tourism offers for positive economic, environmental, and social benefits for tomorrow will depend on the decisions being made today. We can plan well for the development of tourism by adhering to important principles, policies, and philosophies of sustainable tourism or let it happen haphazardly and hope for the best. If we do not define clear-cut directions for sustainable tourism at this juncture in the growth of tourism, there may never be another chance.

We have a limited environment to work with, and much of the environment is already under siege from the many different industrial, technological, and unplanned tourism developments under way. To preserve these resources, to impact the social values of the community, and to add to the quality of life of local citizens worldwide and at the same time elicit favorable economic benefits for tourism is indeed a challenge. This book provides new information, concepts, and policies to help us chart a favorable course of action for tourism to meet those challenges over the next several years.

Sustainable tourism links the planning functions with the social goals of tourism into a concrete set of guidelines to give us direction as we move ahead. Without such guidance we might find tourism's future considerably less beneficial than we hope. With the information and precepts presented in this book, students, travelers, and professionals will have a complete set of conceptual tools for understanding the myriad factors that impact the future of the tourism industry and help ensure its growth in positive ways.

In writing this book, the author has drawn from his rich and varied background as a former governmental policymaker in tourism, a professor of tourism, and a tourism businessperson. As you read this best practices book on sustainable tourism you will see his passionate interests in the well-being of the tourism industry. He strongly believes that responsibly managed tourism is the key to a quality tourism industry in the future.

Stanley Selengut
President
Sustainable Development, Inc.
St. John, U.S. Virgin Islands

Preface

The tourism stage in the twenty-first century presents profound challenges to all actors involved in the tourism industry. Consumers of tourism in the new millennium are demanding greater quality in their tourism products. They want new and different destinations, greater variety, and more flexibility in their travels. Increasingly tourists are expressing a desire for a clean environment, nature tourism, ecotourism, adventurous activities, and more culture, heritage, history, arts, and rural settings.[1] In response, more destinations have become interested in developing higher-quality tourism products and have placed greater emphasis on the natural environment and the built environment, which includes historic, heritage, and cultural sites. Furthermore, business, government, academia, not-for-profit, and local tourism leaders are now likelier to focus their attention on the need to develop and promote tourism sustainability based on preserving the resources on which tourism's success depends. They want to manage sustainable tourism as a legacy to ensure that their children and future generations can enjoy a wide variety of tourism products. The result has been that today's tourism products are more concerned with being compatible with the environment, both natural and constructed. *Managing Sustainable Tourism: A Legacy for the Future* stresses that positive sustainable tourism development is dependent on forward-looking policies and new management philosophies that seek harmonious relations between local communities, the private sector, not-for-profit organizations, academic institutions, and governments at all levels to develop practices that protect natural, built, and cultural environments in a way compatible with economic growth.

The concept of sustainability as a resource development and management philosophy is permeating all levels of policy and practice relating to tourism, from local to global. Sustainable tourism management of the natural and physical environment must, more than ever before, coexist with the economic, sociocultural, health, safety, and security objectives of localities and nations. Finding a balance between economic growth and the protection of natural and built resources is challenging governments and businesses alike to cooperate. The tourism community faces the additional broad challenge of cooperation to support sustainable tourism; in particular, cooperation is necessary among small businesses and local communities who compete at the local level but who wish to attract a broader segment of the market from greater distances. To further explain the dynamic relationship involving *coop*eration at the local level to meet the comp*etition* in the broader tourism market, I earlier developed the concept of *coopetition* (Edgell and Haenisch 1995).[2] *Coopetition* has numerous applications in managing sustainable tourism resources, a few of which will be mentioned in this book.

Managing tourism sustainability as an approach to maintaining and improving the natural and built environments while preserving local culture and heritage is becoming fundamental to a quality tourism product, as reflected in the tourism agendas and programs of seminars, meetings, conferences, articles, and books. A London-based publication titled the *Journal of Sustainable Tourism* became available to the European tourism community in 1993. In 1998, the first Center for Sustainable Tourism in the United States was established at the University of Colorado at Boulder. By 2001, Business Enterprises for Sustainable Travel in New York was publishing *Best Practices,* a journal that highlights successful business practices in sustainable travel. In 2002, Conservation International and *National Geographic Traveler* magazine created the World Legacy Awards, which recognize businesses, organizations, and places that have made an outstanding contribution to promoting the principles of sustainable tourism. By 2003, the National Geographic Society included a special unit devoted to sustainable tourism headed by a Director of Sustainable Tourism. Then, in March 2004, *National Geographic Traveler* published a set of criteria against which it evaluated numerous global tourism destinations' adherence to best practices in sustainable tourism development (Tourtellot 2004). These same criteria were used to evaluate national parks in Canada and the United States, as reported in the July/August 2005 *National Geographic Traveler* (Tourtellot 2005). As a final example, *Managing Sustainable Tourism: A Legacy for the Future* was published to provide educators, students, tourists, governments, and practitioners with a well-grounded explanation of sustainable tourism, to shed light on the important debates taking place in tourism sustainability, and to demonstrate the importance of managing sustainable tourism.

This book addresses many of the major issues in sustainable tourism management and provides ten case studies of past, present, and future interests in sustainable tourism. The aim is to provide proactive prescriptions for achieving tourism growth in a manner that sustains the natural and built environments and preserves the values and beliefs of the local community. The book emphasizes strategic planning as the principal management tool to achieve the goal of tourism sustainability in an ever-changing environment. It is an excellent guide for developers, strategists, educators, planners, policymakers, politicians, activists, managers, entrepreneurs, investors, communicators, students, and citizens interested in quality tourism products. This book looks to the future, taking the long view that positive sustainable tourism is the important goal in the new millennium.

Acknowledgments

I wish to acknowledge that *Managing Sustainable Tourism: A Legacy for the Future* is the culmination of over twenty-five years of research, observation, and discussions with a multitude of people within and outside the tourism industry. The people, organizations, and businesses that have influenced the preparation of this book are too numerous to mention. I appreciate the many friends and colleagues who have patiently given their time and passed on their knowledge over the years to make a book of this scope possible.

Acknowledgment is made to the World Tourism Organization, the Earth Council, the World Travel and Tourism Council, Business Enterprises for Sustainable Travel, the National Geographic Society, the Organization of American States, the Commission for Environmental Cooperation, the Caribbean Tourism Organization, the Travel Industry Association of America, the case study sites, and many other organizations and individuals for their documents, materials, and information. Every effort has been made to identify the sources of such information throughout the text.

I want to thank Scott Allegrucci, Frederick L. Baehner, Jane Barr, M.L. Bass, Dr. Srikanth Beldona, Terry Berggren, Richard L. Berkley, Dr. Keith Betts, Dr. Kristen Betts, Judy Billing, Becky Blake, Douglas R. Brindley, Margie Brooks, Kathy D. Brown, Ambassador Frederick M. Bush, Avna Paiewonsky Cassinelli, Dr. Thoric Cederstrom, Dr. James A. Chandler, Dr. Rosina C. Chia, Dr. Suzanne D. Cook, Dr. John C. Crotts, Louis J. D'Amore, Sarah Dalton, Bernadette Davis, Peter de Blanc, Dr. Nancy Del Risco, Dr. John J. Edgell Jr., Linda Edgell, Richard M. Edgell, JoAnna Edgerton, Jim Ensor, Ron Erdmann, Dr. Sylvia Escott-Stump, Ted Lee Eubanks Jr., Dr. Dori Finley, Romeo Fleming, Dr. William A. Forsythe, Dr. Douglas Frechtling, Dr. Joseph D. Fridgen, Maryanne B. Friend, Dr. Margie Gallagher, Dr. Bill C. Gartner, Dean Emeritus Chuck Y. Gee, Martha Glass, Tom Glennon, Terry Golden, Rodney Gust, Marty Hackney, Todd Haenisch, Linda Harbaugh, Bill Hardman, Dr. Donald E. Hawkins, Jason Hilgers, Dr. Brian J. Hill, Daniel B. Hoerz, Jean S.

Holder, Dean Karla Hughes, Dr. Min Hyun, Dr. Jafar Jafari, Dr. Janne Jorgensen, Dr. John T. Kalberer, Michael Kelly, Dr. Lauriston R. King, Bonnie Kogos, Dr. Bernard Lane, Lynn Lewis, Ron Logan, Dr. Patrick T. Long, Carol S. Lohr, I. Katherine Magruder, Dr. James C. Makens, Helen N. Marano, Chikako S. Massey, Dr. Hannah Messerli, Lynn D. Minges, Ing. Raul Nieto Morales, Margaret (Peggy) Novotny, Dr. Ronald H. Nowaczyk, David Parker, Tom Penney, Sarah Lilley Phelps, Dr. Abraham Pizam, Dr. Rick Purdue, Clayton P. Reid, Edward F. Reilly Jr., John Robinson, Dr. Kenneth I. Rubin, Kurtis M. Ruf, Dr. Timothy J. Runyan, Carl Sage, Dr. Pauline Sheldon, J. Carl Smith, Jay G. Smith, Kay Smith, Dr. Eduardo Fayos-Solá, Dr. Sheryl E. Spivack, Jason R. Swanson, Dr. William Swart, Dr. Marcia Taylor, Anthony J. Tighe, Dr. Rebecca Torres, Cindy Tripp, Dr. Muzaffer Uysal, Debbie G. Vargas, Carla D. Vauthrin, Anthony B. Watkins, Scott Wayne, Glenn Weaver, and Barbara Zurhellen who added, corrected, provided information, talked to me, supported me, and/or otherwise impacted this book in some form or another.

I want to express my appreciation to Jean Arey, Dr. Ginger Smith, Amy Jordan Webb, Sarah J. Gust, Maria DelMastro Allen, and David L. Edgell Jr. for agreeing to read early versions of the manuscript and for giving me their advice, changes, edits, corrections, and support. My special thanks to Sharon Crozier, Sarah J. Gust, and Maria DelMastro Allen for typing many draft versions of this book.

I would like to identify several people who were instrumental through their willingness to help prepare the case studies for this book. I would not have been able to prepare the first case study on "The U.S. Virgin Islands' Newest Sustainable Tourism Product—St. Croix Salt River Bay National Historical Park and Ecological Preserve" without the information and commitment of Jesse K. Thomson and the editing by William F. Cissel. I wish to thank the Ministry of Tourism of Ecuador for information used in the case study on "Ecuador—The Wonderful World of the Galapagos Islands." Debbie Bennett was my benefactor for all the information included in the case study on "Missouri, Big Cedar Lodge—The Epitome of Sustainable Tourism." The case study on "Sustainable Ecotourism Development in the Emberá Indigenous Communities— Chargres National Park, Panama" was not in the first draft of the book; however, Gerald (Jerry) P. Bauer and Jerry Wylie of the U.S.

Department of Agriculture's Forest Service, International Institute of Tropical Forestry, who worked on the project, prepared almost all the information, generously gave me permission to use it, and have been true leaders in ecotourism. Someone who spent endless hours with me in conversations about tourism and who caused me to share her love of the small community of Vandalia, Illinois, is my mother-in-law and wonderful lady Trudy Smith. She spent months collecting, organizing, and editing information for me so that I could write the case study on "Looking for Lincoln—Vandalia, Illinois, Develops New Lincoln Park." I owe a debt of gratitude to the Illinois Historic Preservation Agency and individuals on site at the Cahokia Mounds near Collinsville, Illinois, for showing me the mounds, giving me permission to use their information, and providing other information so I could write the case study on "Early Native Americans—Cahokia Mounds State Historic Site." My thanks go to Cindy Tripp for providing information and Maria DelMastro Allen for helping me develop and construct the case study on "Roanoke River Paddle Trail—A 'Watery' Approach to Rural Tourism." After several visits to the Kansas Tallgrass Prairie National Preserve, and in conversations with site personnel at the preserve, I was able to prepare the case study "A Rural Masterpiece—Kansas Tallgrass Prairie National Preserve." Gail Harrison helped me immensely to locate the appropriate information to prepare the case study on "The Embodiment of Managed Tourism—Canada, Banff National Park."

Finally, special thanks go to Sarah J. Gust for her help in researching sustainable tourism sites in Kansas, Illinois, Wyoming (in the United States), Belize, Costa Rica, France, Scotland, Spain, St. Martin, and the United Kingdom. She was also instrumental in reviewing some of the case studies and making changes in the manuscript of this book in 2003, 2004, and 2005.

This book would not have been possible without all the hard work and dedication of the staff at The Haworth Press. I especially want to thank Patricia Brown, Rebecca Browne, Anissa Harper, Jillian Mason-Possemato, Peg Marr, Amy Rentner, Josh R. Ribacove, Tracy Sayles, and Lora Wiggins.

Every attempt has been made to make this book accurate and informational. References and quotations are appropriately acknowledged as carefully as possible. Any errors or omissions are the sole responsibility of the author.

Chapter 1

Tourism Today and Tomorrow

Coming events cast their shadows before.

Thomas Campbell, "Lochiel's Warning"

INTRODUCTION

Tourism in the third millennium, properly managed, has the potential to participate in, change, and improve the social, cultural, economic, political, and ecological dimensions of future lifestyles. In this new millennium, one of the highest purposes of the policies and philosophies of tourism will be to integrate the economic, political, cultural, intellectual, and environmental benefits of tourism for people, destinations, and countries, resulting in a higher quality of life.[1] Charting a course for tourism in the future will demand new ways of looking at all attributes of tourism—but most important, its sustainability. In this book, I suggest that

> Sustainable tourism, properly managed, can become a major vehicle for the realization of humankind's highest aspirations in the quest to achieve economic prosperity while maintaining social, cultural, and environmental integrity.

Managing Sustainable Tourism: A Legacy for the Future explores many proactive goals, objectives, policies, and strategies aimed at the protection, enrichment, and enhancement of the natural and built environments, resulting in economic prosperity and overall improvement of the quality of life of the local citizenry.

Humankind has always traveled for one purpose or another. A million years ago, travel was primarily related to survival through hunting, fishing, and food gathering. Our early ancestors often traveled to

1

follow a herd of animals, migrating to new areas where they sought
safety and security and could obtain food and water. Later, explorers
and traders, such as the Phoenicians, traveled to new areas of the
world, establishing travel trade routes. Other societies, such as the
Greeks, traveled to learn about other cultures and to enjoy new scenic
beauty. The Romans traveled as part of their military conquests and in
the process built substantial roads and established recreation areas
and accommodations for their soldiers. Marco Polo led Europeans
into a whole new world of cultural travel and set the stage for future
travelers, adventurers, and explorers to document their travels, as he
did in the book *The Travels of Marco Polo* (or, *The Description of the
World*). Christopher Columbus was fascinated by the tales in Marco
Polo's book and was convinced he could find a new route to the riches
of the Far East. A little-known author and explorer, and possibly the
first Englishman in the "New World" to describe nature-based travel
or ecotourism, was John Lawson, who documented his observations
of flora, fauna, and Native American culture during his travels
throughout "Carolina" (now North and South Carolina) (Lawson
1709/1967). Meriwether Lewis and William Clark kept a detailed
journal of their travels, adding a clear dimension to the study of natural habitat, flora, fauna, and Native American culture. Later, Charles
Darwin made scientific observations about the environment of the
Galapagos Islands that led to his theory of evolution as documented
in *The Origin of Species*. He also wrote a book about his travels, *The
Voyage of the Beagle*, which is a classic travel book and history of
tourism sustainability. Yuri Gagarin, the first Russian space traveler,
opened up a new era of travel that is only now beginning to be
understood.

Travel has played a vital role in the development of civilizations.[2]
Discoveries of new lands and trade routes, and exchanges of cultures
and knowledge, have all rested on the ability to travel. In this new age
of tourism with multiple products to choose from, around half the
world's population will travel for one reason or another. Some people
travel for business, some for pleasure, and some to participate in special sports, artistic, musical, historical, religious, and outdoor events.
As tourism continues to take advantage of the great strides being
made in transport and communication technologies, individuals will
have better opportunities to understand their own natural environment and cultural surroundings as well as those of other people and

nations. It is the environment—natural habitats, built structures, culture, heritage, history, and social interactions—that will sustain tourism as a legacy for future generations. It is the management of these sustaining resources that will be the lifeblood of future tourism.

New changes in tourism for the new millennium suggest that new philosophies, concepts, principles, practices, and issues will define the parameters of sustainable tourism.[3] A management philosophy that provides guidance and direction in sustainable tourism development is just beginning to emerge. The concept of utilizing sustainable tourism development to stimulate economic growth but maintain the natural and built environment is receiving greater attention in industry and government. Such principles of tourism sustainability are emerging simultaneously from industry, government, and academia. For example, in 1998, the tourism community in the State of Colorado caucused at the University of Colorado at Boulder to establish the Center for Sustainable Tourism (the first in the United States), to be housed in the School of Business. This center serves as a "virtual think tank" where students, faculty, tourism industry representatives, community leaders, and government officials who are committed to the intelligent and orderly growth of tourism can share their concerns, ideas, research, and solutions. In 1999, under the auspices of the North American Free Trade Agreement, the Commission for Environmental Cooperation convoked "A Dialogue on Sustainable Tourism in Natural Areas in North America," in Montreal, Canada. In 2000, Dr. Ginger Smith of The George Washington University delivered an interesting paper titled "Environmental and Cultural Sustainability: Tourism Promotion in the New Millennium" at the "International Conference 2000: Cultural Tourism in the New Millennium," in Kwangju City, Korea (Smith 2000). The National Park System Advisory Board Report (2001), *Rethinking the National Parks for the 21st Century,* also speaks of "principles of sustainability" and encourages educational programs and related forums to talk about history, biodiversity, preservation, native cultures, and other concepts of sustainability, which are core to future quality tourism. In 2002, Dutch St. Maarten (with support from French St. Martin) held its "First Annual Conference on Sustainable Development: Environmental and Social Impacts of the Global Tourism Industry." In 2003, the National Geographic Society and *National Geographic Traveler* magazine launched several new efforts in sustainable tourism. A special sustainable tourism conference, "Green Hotel Conference: Opening the Door to a Greener Future," was held in Montego Bay, Jamaica, in 2004. In 2005, some East Carolina University personnel in Greenville, North Carolina, embarked on a number of new sustainable tourism endeavors, including special research for this book.

Other new developments in sustainable tourism have arisen as a result of past lessons learned in the tourism industry. For example, the focus of tourism in the 1970s was almost always economic development, growth, and financial gain. By the 1980s, it was clear that tourism projects must not only include an economic impact statement but also meet new and growing environmental regulations. By the 1990s, it was clear that a third dimension needed to be added, that of social impact, particularly on local communities. The social dimension often relates to history, heritage, and culture and requires progressive local government involvement and public participation. In the new millennium, we are witnessing a strong movement toward the management of all three elements—economic, environmental, and social—as a condition of sustainable tourism.

To me, the simplest definition of sustainable tourism is achieving quality growth in a manner that does not deplete the natural and built environment and preserves the culture, history, and heritage of the local community. In the context of this book, the word *environment,* as it relates to sustainable tourism (unless otherwise explained), refers to natural habitats, built structures, culture, heritage, history, and social interactions. Managing sustainable tourism in the new millennium depends on forward-looking policies and sound management philosophies, including a harmonious relationship between local communities, the private sector, and governments in developmental practices that protect natural, built, and cultural environments in a way compatible with economic growth. This book explores the dynamics of these relationships.

THE WORLD OF TOURISM

Tourism is big business. Travel expenditures today are a major source of income and employment for many nations. Global tourism provides employment for more than 222 million people worldwide, or approximately one in every twelve workers. Domestic and international tourism is an industry worth approximately $4.7 trillion globally, and this figure will continue to grow. World Travel and Tourism Council (2005) projections suggest that the tourism industry will generate $7.8 trillion by 2015, providing more than 269 million jobs. Also of importance is the realization by the industry that the future of tourism depends on its development being in harmony with concerns for the environment and culture.

A report from the North American Free Trade Agreement's Commission for Environmental Cooperation in 2000 mentioned that nature-based tourism accounts for between 10 and 15 percent of all international travel expenditures. The World Tourism Organization[4] suggests that ecotourism and all nature-related forms of tourism account for approximately 20 percent of total inbound travel (visits to a country by nonresidents) (Commission for Environmental Cooperation 2000). Such travel has become so significant that the United Nations designated 2002 the International Year of Ecotourism. Culture-based tourism, nature-based tourism, heritage tourism, adventure tourism, and geotourism are all important components of sustainable tourism. Cultural tourism assets, as a part of sustainable tourism, include museums, art galleries, historical theme parks, music events, local cuisine, dance, theater, and arts festivals. In the same context, ecotourism includes those aspects of tourism based upon a relatively undisturbed natural area, with an emphasis on the protection of the area's fauna and flora.

Looking at international tourism only (i.e., excluding the larger component, domestic tourism), the World Tourism Organization (2005) reported that more than 760 million people traveled internationally in 2004. Estimated international tourism receipts for the same period exceeded $622 billion (excluding expenditures of more than $65 billion for international air transport). For many years, international tourism has shown a healthy growth rate. Over the past ten years, worldwide international tourist arrivals have grown at an average rate of more than 5 percent per year, and, more significant, international tourism receipts have grown at an average rate of more than 12 percent. Although the September 11, 2001, tragedy in the United States temporarily slowed global travel in late 2001 and early 2002, travel had already started to recover by the end of 2002. The Iraqi war in 2003 and 2004 also dampened international travel, but by the beginning of 2005 there were strong indications that tourism was again on a positive growth path.

CHARTING A NEW COURSE
FOR SUSTAINABLE TOURISM

A clean, healthy, and protected environment, apart from being inherently good for tourism, is also key to its competitiveness. Increasingly, consumers of tourism are willing to pay more for a cleaner environment. An important survey by the Travel Industry Association of America (2003a) found that 83 percent of travelers would support companies that have good environmental practices. Moreover, the survey showed that travelers would spend 6.2 percent more on average for travel services and products offered by environmentally friendly companies.[5]

The bottom line is that the environment is the tourism industry's most important resource. Whether tourists are just lying on a beach, diving, whale watching, hiking, biking, or visiting sites and attractions, the environment is the essence of most tourism products. It is the experience and enjoyment of the environment that the tourism industry markets. Ecosystems (such as reefs, forests, arctic tundra, rivers, coasts, islands, plains, lakes, mountains), flora and fauna, and cultural, historical, heritage, and arts sites are all important attractions for vacationers. Almost no other industry is as environmentally dependent as the tourism industry. Therefore, it is imperative that we take the necessary steps to ensure the protection and enhancement of the natural and built environment and cultural heritage through sustainable tourism management. Put simply, sustainable tourism management systems can increase the capacity of these sites to accommodate quality tourism with limited or no degradation.

Choosing a management approach or a combination of approaches can be a complex process that requires evaluation of economic, environmental, cultural, heritage, and social policies. The objective is to design the least intrusive form of intervention that results in efficient, effective, and equitable decisions on tourism development and use of natural and built resources. The goal of sustainable tourism management, whether in the public or private arena, is to choose one or more approaches that foster practical, acceptable, and profitable tourism enterprises while preventing damage to the built and natural environment. These choices become critical in determining long-term tourism sustainability.

New and innovative approaches to resolving sustainable tourism issues are also emerging. For example, in 1995, the World Tourism Organization and the World Travel and Tourism Council joined forces with the Earth Council to promote an action plan to improve the environment and make the tourism sector more sustainable. This action plan is referred to as "Agenda 21 for the Travel and Tourism Industry: Toward Environmentally Sustainable Development," and was launched in October 1995, in London, England. It establishes a systematic framework for action in the twenty-first century, outlining main priority areas for governments and a ten-step program for business to make the tourism industry more environmentally responsible.[6] By 2005, many good examples existed of positive movements in sustainable tourism in certain areas of the world, including, to my knowledge, areas of these countries and territories: Australia, Austria, the Bahamas, Barbados, Belize, Bonaire (Netherlands Antilles), Brazil, British Virgin Islands, Canada, Chile, Costa Rica, Cuba, the Czech Republic, Dominica, Ecuador, Egypt, Fiji, France, Gabon, Germany, Greece, Guatemala, Ireland, Italy, Jamaica, Japan, Jeju Island (Republic of Korea), Jordan, Kenya, Mexico, Morocco, Nepal, New Zealand, Norway, Peru, Poland, Portugal, Russia, Scotland, South Africa, Spain, St. Lucia and St. Vincent, St. Maarten, St. Martin, Switzerland, Tanzania, Turkey, the United Kingdom, the United States, and the U.S. Virgin Islands.[7]

In 2002, another term, "geotourism," was introduced into sustainable tourism by Jonathan B. Tourtellot, in "The Hidden Clout of Travelers" in the May/June 2002 issue of *National Geographic Traveler* magazine. He defines it as "tourism that sustains or enhances the geographic character of the place being visited—its environment, culture, aesthetics, heritage, and the well-being of its residents." Although the emphasis of geotourism is on the geographical character of the place being visited, it also includes concepts generally included in definitions of "sustainable tourism."

In 2003, *National Geographic Traveler* and the Travel Industry Association of America sponsored a two-part study titled *Geotourism: The New Trend in Travel.* This report showed that more than three-quarters of American travelers feel it is important that their visits do not damage the environment; 62 percent said it is important to learn about other cultures when they travel, and 38 percent said they would pay more to use a travel company that strives to protect and preserve the environment.[8]

A study in 2005 of the North Carolina seacoast (Edgell 2005) (sponsored by a North Carolina Sea Grant and conducted by the Institute for Tourism at East Carolina University) found varying degrees of concern for sustainable tourism initiatives along the coastline. The March 2004 issue of *National Geographic Traveler* gave the Outer Banks coastline of North Carolina a low ranking in terms of sustainable tourism (Tourtellot 2004). This acted as a wake-up call, and the Outer Banks has already embarked on several new projects that are supportive of sustainable tourism.

Increasingly, one can find good examples of hotels, resorts, and other tourism businesses taking action to protect the natural and built environment. In the April 1999 issue of *ISdesigNET Magazine,* Janet Wiens mentions a hotel example: the Sheraton Rittenhouse Square Hotel in Philadelphia. Opened in 1999, the property is dubbed as the first environmentally smart hotel in the United States. The material and fabrics found on the property are produced without toxic bleaches or dyes. All paint, wallpaper, carpeting, and draperies contain no toxic chemicals. The furniture is constructed from wood from managed forests. This shows that hotels in urban locations can help preserve the planet. Many other positive examples of sustainability exist, a few of which are included as case studies in this book.

Forms of recognition for entities that subscribe to the good management of sustainable tourism are evolving. An important step forward was the announcement in 2002 by Conservation International and *National Geographic Traveler* of the World Legacy Awards for Sustainable Tourism. These awards recognize outstanding businesses, organizations, and places that have made a significant contribution toward promoting the principles of sustainable tourism. These principles include the conservation of nature, economic benefit to local peoples, and respect for cultural diversity. Winners are to be chosen in four categories: nature travel, heritage tourism, destination stewardship, and general purpose hotels and resorts.

I have included in this book particular case studies that demonstrate positive sustainable tourism practices that are becoming increasingly popular. These case studies are intended to expand the reader's comprehension of the great variety of approaches to sustainable tourism development. No single model can describe the many different circumstances encountered in sustainable tourism development. Rather, these case studies are simply some examples of positive progress in attempting to manage sustainable tourism in the new millennium.

OVERVIEW OF CHAPTERS

This first chapter is a broad-brush sketch of sustainable tourism and the size of the tourism industry. It suggests that managing sustainable tourism in the third millennium will be a critical step for the growth and well-being of tourism. It ends with a case study of "The U.S. Virgin Islands' Newest Sustainable Tourism Project—St. Croix Salt River Bay National Historical Park and Ecological Preserve," which is a positive embodiment of many of the elements of sustainable tourism. It is also a good illustration of the impact that a small number of involved and concerned local citizens can have on a project that has local, national, and international implications.

Chapter 2 sets the stage for understanding sustainable tourism. It raises important policy questions and issues for consideration in the future. Positive attributes of sustainable tourism are presented. Some sustainable tourism concepts and principles are introduced. An interesting case study, "Ecuador—The Wonderful World of the Galapagos Islands," is included at the end of the chapter.

Chapter 3 discusses the economic viability of sustainable tourism development and the local tourism concerns where the impact is greatest. It also addresses the important issue of marketing sustainable tourism. The case study on "Missouri, Big Cedar Lodge—The Epitome of Sustainable Tourism" demonstrates the positive example of a resort that understands the value of sustainable tourism development.

Chapter 4 discusses nature-based tourism as an important component of sustainable tourism. It makes special reference to environmental concerns in the natural environment. The case study, "Sustainable Ecotourism Development in the Emberá Indigenous Communities—Chagres National Park, Panama," is a very special example of what can be accomplished with good leadership and direction.

Chapter 5 introduces heritage tourism as an important part of sustainable tourism. It refers to the beginning of heritage tourism, defines the concept, and suggests a model. The case study, "Looking for Lincoln—Vandalia, Illinois, Develops New Lincoln Park," looks at what a small rural community has accomplished in terms of heritage tourism.

Chapter 6 addresses the cultural aspects of tourism. It describes cultural tourism, gives some examples, and suggests its importance as part of sustainable tourism. The case study, "Early Native Americans—Cahokia Mounds State Historic Site," discusses one of the most important archaeological tourism sites in the United States.

Chapter 7 suggests that rural tourism is a key ingredient in sustainability. The chapter details the importance of rural tourism and the challenge of developing sustainable tourism in rural areas. The case study, "Roanoke River Paddle Trail—A 'Watery' Approach to Rural Tourism," illustrates a farsighted approach to recreational opportunities along a river consistent with supporting the ecosystem and natural beauty.

Chapter 8 presents guidelines that give direction to, and a rationale for, sustainable tourism. It suggests what will work at the local level. The case study, "A Rural Masterpiece—Kansas Tallgrass Prairie National Preserve," demonstrates the way in which important cooperation over a national park is developing sustainable tourism.

In Chapter 9 some problems in tourism sustainability are explored. Management ideas are introduced, and a case is made for effective management as the answer to the sustainability of tourism. The case study, "The Embodiment of Managed Tourism—Canada, Banff National Park," is an example of positive sustainable tourism management.

Chapter 10 finally challenges the reader to think carefully through the concepts of sustainable tourism. It also identifies some of the future issues in tourism that will affect our ability to manage tourism sustainability into the next century. The case study, "Sustainable Tourism in the U.S. Virgin Islands, St. John—Maho Bay, Harmony, and Concordia," explains the merging of ecotourism and heritage tourism into a sustainable tourism model.

CASE STUDY: THE U.S. VIRGIN ISLANDS'
NEWEST SUSTAINABLE TOURISM PRODUCT—
ST. CROIX SALT RIVER BAY NATIONAL
HISTORICAL PARK AND ECOLOGICAL PRESERVE

St. Croix is located in the Caribbean Sea, 1,500 miles south of New York City and 1,100 miles southeast of Miami, and is imbued with a rich cultural mix, an interesting history, and a special heritage. The first Secretary of the Treasury for the United States, Alexander Hamilton, grew up in St. Croix. St. Croix is the largest of the three major islands that comprise the U.S. Virgin Islands. It is an important business center for the islands and also has a well-established tourism industry with a full range of accommodations from large hotels to small intimate guest houses—as well as a four-berth cruise ship dock in Frederiksted.

Salt River Bay in St. Croix provides a unique case study of sustainable tourism. It has natural, archaeological, and historical significance. Prehistoric and colonial-era archeological sites and ruins are found in a dynamic, tropical ecosystem that supports endangered species. Salt River Bay also represents what dedicated local citizens can accomplish in terms of sustainable tourism development.[9]

Salt River Bay was first settled and developed in the period AD 50 to 650 by Neolithic (New Stone Age) farmers known to archaeologists as the Pre-Taino or Igneri. These Amerindian people, as well as the later Taino and Callinago (Island Caribs), practiced slash-and-burn agriculture. The archaeological evidence found at Columbus Landing Site includes bird, fish, rodent, and turtle bones, crab claws, and shellfish, indicating that all of these Amerindian peoples were also hunters and gatherers.[10]

Analysis of pottery found at Columbus Landing Site indicates that changes occurred from within the Virgin Islands and from without. By AD 1200, the cultural transition that began around AD 700 ended with the growing influence of the Taino. Their settlement at Columbus Landing Site is marked by a stone petroglyph that depicts a ceremonial ball court or "batey" (the only one of its kind found in the Lesser Antilles) and characteristic pottery.

Some time before the arrival of Christopher Columbus, the Island Caribs seized St. Croix. During the Carib domination of St. Croix, the Caribs raided eastern Puerto Rico and captured Tainos as slaves. Irregular warfare for the purpose of obtaining captives and plunder was an important facet of Carib culture.

On November 14, 1493, on his second voyage to the "New World," Columbus came upon the island that the Tainos called AyAy ("the river") and the Caribs referred to as Cibuquiera ("the stony land"). He was to name it Santa Cruz or "Holy Cross." Columbus sent armed men ashore to explore the Carib village and to search for fresh water on the west side of Salt River Bay. The men seized Taino slaves before returning from the village to the flagship anchored outside of the bay. The Spaniards rammed a Carib canoe and a fierce skirmish ensued. One Carib and one Spaniard were killed. This conflict is the first documented example of Native American resistance to European encroachment.

After some limited attempts at peace between the Spaniards and Caribs, a Spanish adventurer raided St. Croix for slaves, capturing as many as 140 Caribs. Carib resistance to Spanish enslavement and the Caribs' participation in the Taino uprising in Puerto Rico were used by the Spanish to justify their extermination. By 1590, the Caribs had left and St. Croix was unpopulated.

The seventeenth century saw several unsuccessful attempts to settle St. Croix by various groups of Europeans, including the English, the Dutch, the Spanish again, the French, and the French Chapter of the Knights of Malta. Each of these groups left its special mark on St. Croix, adding to the unique culture, history, and heritage of the island. After Denmark purchased St. Croix from France in 1733, the island developed into an important agricultural and trade center. The purchase of the Danish West Indies (including St. Croix) by the United States in 1917 for military strategic purposes also formalized an economic relationship with the U.S. mainland that continues to this day.

Public Law 102-247 established the Salt River Bay National Historical Park and Ecological Preserve on February 24, 1992. It was officially dedicated on November 13, 1993, the 500th anniversary of the arrival of Columbus off Salt River. Salt River encompasses the entire spectrum of human history in the West Indies.[11] In addition to being a historical and cultural site, the current 1,015-acre Salt River Park, inclusive of 600 acres of water, is an important ecosystem. Its natural significance and beauty derive from the combination of upland terrestrial, estuary, and open marine environments within a relatively small geographic area. It encompasses the single largest mangrove system remaining in the Virgin Islands. The designation of the Salt River Bay area as a national park helps to assure its sustainability for future generations. The legislative mandates are to protect the cultural and natural resources within the park boundaries, to interpret their significance and value to the public, and to encourage scientific research.

The national park concept was strengthened in 2004 with the purchase from private owners of a hilltop house that overlooks the landing site of Christopher Columbus. The site will house the National Park Services Visitor Contact Station and Interpretive Center. This land was added to the Salt River Bay National Historical Park and Ecological Preserve by Congressional authorization, bringing to an end a ten-year effort to buy the eight-and-a-half-acre tract.

Chapter 2

A Philosophic Approach
to Sustainable Tourism

[T]ourism in the twenty-first century will be a major vehicle for
fulfilling people's aspiration for a higher quality of life . . . tourism also has the potential to be one of the most important stimu-
lants for global improvement in the social, cultural, economic,
political and ecological dimensions of future lifestyles.

David L. Edgell Sr., *International Tourism Policy,* 1990

SUSTAINABLE TOURISM DOMINATES OUR FUTURE

As defined in Chapter 1, sustainable tourism means achieving
growth in a manner that does not deplete the natural and built environment and preserves the culture, history, heritage, and arts of the
local community. Within this concept is increasing recognition that
sustainable management of resources will lead to acceptable conservation and the development of a higher-quality tourism product. Human beings can use and modify the environment in positive (and negative) ways. In summary, managing sustainable tourism can effectively
enhance and enrich the environment.

Key elements of tourism sustainability include meeting the needs
of both visitors and host communities and protecting and enhancing
the tourism attraction for the future as part of a national economic resource. The relationship between tourists, host communities, businesses, attractions, and the environment is complex, interactive, and
symbiotic.

Funding and obtaining political and policy acceptance of sustainable tourism development can be problematic; however, recently,
public and private cooperation has produced innovative strategies to

respond to these concerns.[1] For example, admission charges to natural and historic places can be made commensurate with their uniqueness, thereby providing for self-funded site maintenance and improvements and the moderation of use. Additional economic questions are addressed in Chapter 3.

Sensitivity to the environment is rapidly becoming a major component of international tourism marketing strategies; too often we see incidents where visitors are insensitive to their surroundings, suggesting that tourists and the environment may not, in some respects, be entirely compatible. Some tourists want such souvenirs as unusual corals, exotic rocks, or colorful seashells. Others trample irreplaceable tundra or otherwise alter natural flora, which can compound the biological damage to other plants and animals. Others still are tempted to chip off a fragment of an American Indian abode, steal native artifacts, or otherwise desecrate fabricated objects of historical and artistic significance.

The environment with which tourism interacts includes not only land, air, water, flora, and fauna, but also history, culture, and heritage. The responsible tourist should become informed in order to adapt to societal and environmental differences, especially when traveling abroad. The protected natural environment is often what attracts tourists to a specific destination, and sometimes the greater the mixture of natural environmental elements in a single trip, from rain forests to ruins to river rafting, the deeper and more memorable is the experience. In many respects the attraction is the ecosystem, the wildlife, the rich archeological discoveries, the climate, or the culture that the tourist may have read about or seen on the television screen. The important message is that through educational programs, awareness, and controlled visitation, the natural environment as a tourist attraction can be nurtured, managed, and protected for future generations to enjoy.

One U.S. state making rapid progress in researching, developing, and promoting sustainable tourism is North Carolina, which has a number of unique sustainable tourism products in its western mountains, in its central region, and on its eastern coast. It also has rich tourism resources, often unrecognized, throughout its rural areas. One special example is Cape Lookout, which, as part of the National Seashore in North Carolina, is operated by the National Park Service, U.S. Department of the Interior. The flora and the fauna, including a population of wild horses that have adapted to their environment over the past few hundred years, are protected. Cape Lookout National Seashore is a constantly changing environment that, when left relatively undisturbed by humans, maintains a natural balance. The National Park Service issues visitor guidelines and pamphlets on topics from beach safety (sun, heat, and swimming information) and survival tips (poisonous animals and plants) to a special program to make the park "trash free." Volunteers from across the country vie for the opportunity to help maintain the Cape Lookout Lighthouse, staff its visitor center, and reside in the light keeper's quarters during their tenure. Probably no better example can be found nationally of the National Park Service (2005) implementing its mission statement:

> [T]o promote and regulate the use of the . . . national parks . . . which purpose is to conserve the scenery and the natural and historic objects and the wild life therein and to provide for the enjoyment of the same in such manner and by such means as will leave them unimpaired for the enjoyment of future generations.

The Service is also responsible for managing a great variety of national and international programs designed to help extend the benefits of natural and cultural resource conservation and outdoor recreation throughout this country and the world.

Another excellent example of sustainable tourism at the local level in North Carolina is the Pitt County canoe/kayak paddle trails system, a collaboration among several different groups and many volunteers, including the Mid-East Resource Conservation and Development Council, Inc., the Cypress Group of the Sierra Club, the Pamlico-Tar River Foundation, and the Pitt County Board of Commissioners, with some funding provided through grants from the Adopt-A-Trail program and the National Recreational Trails program administered by the North Carolina Division of Parks and Recreation. The organizers have produced an informative trail map, researched and marked many of the historic sites along the river trail, and prepared guidelines to help the participants better enjoy the experience and, at the same time, preserve the area. This venture also demonstrates that diverse groups with active members can cooperate to develop and manage excellent sustainable tourism resources.

WHAT TO LOOK FOR IN SUSTAINABLE TOURISM

Sustainable tourism can be difficult to define, describe, and measure because it must relate today's dynamic tourism needs to tomorrow's concern for the future. Tony Griffin and Nicolette Boele's (1993) article "Alternative Paths to Sustainable Tourism" outlines the following five key elements for tourism sustainability:

1. Preserving the current resource base for future generations
2. Maintaining the productivity of the resource base
3. Maintaining biodiversity and avoiding irreversible environmental changes
4. Ensuring equity within and between generations
5. Maintaining and protecting the heritage (culture and history) of the area, region, or nation[2]

The challenge is finding an acceptable balance among these elements. The different business and consumer interests in tourism often overlook the sustainability aspect of tourism; hosts and guests often see the tourism environment through different glasses.

In March 2004, the *National Geographic Traveler* magazine compiled the world's first "Index of Destination Stewardship," which ranked tourism sustainability in 115 world destinations (Tourtellot 2004). The magazine worked with National Geographic's Sustainable Tourism Initiative and a team from Leeds Metropolitan University in the United Kingdom to conduct this complex global survey. The global "Leeds" panel (which included me) comprised over 200 experts in a variety of fields—ecology, sustainable tourism, geography, urban and regional planning, travel writing and photography, historic preservation, cultural anthropology, archaeology, and related disciplines. Most were seasoned travelers and generally had good evaluation skills. They were asked to rate each destination they had personally visited recently, based on the following six criteria:

1. environmental and ecological quality
2. social and cultural integrity
3. condition of any historic building and archaeological sites
4. aesthetic appeal
5. quality of tourism management, and
6. the outlook for the future

The results of the survey were divided into three general categories, "The Good," "Not So Good," and "Getting Ugly," which became the subtitles of the published article by Jonathan Tourtellot (2004). The pronouncement was quite revealing, and surprising to many of the destinations and to many in the travel world. The survey is a good measuring stick and an incentive for destinations to take stock and to seek improvements, where necessary, for the future of their areas. It is likely that similar ratings will follow as travelers seek out destinations that support sustainable tourism practices.

SUSTAINING THE TOURISM PRODUCT

Ecoefficiency in sustainable tourism is a characteristic of those companies and nations that take advantage of the potential success value of incorporating minimum resource use and minimum pollution into public and private sector tourism practices. The New Zealand Ministry of Tourism (1992, p. 8), for example, provides the following description:

> To practice eco-efficiency, tourism developers need to consider the environment creatively, throughout project design, construction and operation. Failure to do so could be costly and cause adverse public attention. Those who are responsible for delivering products and services to the visitor must examine their operations in light of sustainable resource management. This may involve any of the following actions:
>
> Protecting the biosphere
> Reducing and disposing of wastes
> Adopting energy efficient practices
> Minimizing environmental risks
> Undertaking "green" marketing
> Mitigating environmental marketing
> Providing complete and credible environmental information for visitors
> Incorporating environmental values in the management of operations
> Conducting regular environmental audits

Increasing numbers of private, public, and nonprofit entities are recognizing the value of sustainable tourism development and are cooperating in efforts to set aside specific tracts of land for the protection of the natural and built environment. A 1995 *Viewpoint* article titled "Toward a Greener Globe" contains an interesting discussion of the dependence of tourism on the natural and cultural environment (World Travel and Tourism Council 1995). The article suggests that sustainable tourism development "is both morally right and good business" for the world's tourism industry. In brief, the article indicates that much of the world's business community is coming into step with sustainable tourism development as it reflects society's desire to preserve environments and cultures for future generations to enjoy because "our survival depends on a healthy environment" (p. 11).

Global recognition that the natural environment is under severe pressure is growing, and it has crossed political and philosophic borders. The concept of sustainability and stewardship for future generations is attracting widespread support (New Zealand Ministry of Tourism 1992). The development of long-term policies, rather than short-term fixes, is essential to guarantee that tourism growth occurs in a socially, economically, and environmentally responsible manner.

A conceptual statement can be found in the Pacific Asia Travel Association's "Code for Environmentally Responsible Tourism" as follows:

> [Sustainable tourism development] recognizes the necessity to ensure a sustainable future, meets the needs of the tourism industry today, and does not compromise the ability of this and future generations to consume the environment. This Code succinctly describes where many countries and businesses would like to be with respect to an environmental ethic for tourism. (Liu 1994, p. 16)

Contributing to a nation's quality of life through tourism is a sobering challenge. This intellectual transformation will never happen by itself, but only as an integral part of a regimented policy and planning process for the development of tourism based on a greater understanding of the global environment.[3]

BEST PRACTICES TO GUIDE TOURISM'S FUTURE

Modern sustainable tourism policy is a positive approach that seeks to maintain quality tourism products over an extended period in order to meet the demands of the growing domestic and international market for environmental tourism experiences. We have the ability to modify certain aspects of the environment for better or worse. Unless careful policy prescriptions and management tools are in place, tourism can degrade the environment and otherwise diminish its attributes.

A conceptual approach to sustainable tourism development set forth by the World Conservation Union includes four major principles (World Tourism Organization 1993):

1. *Ecological sustainability:* Development is compatible with the maintenance of essential ecological processes, biological diversity, and biological resources.
2. *Cultural sustainability:* Development increases people's control over their lives, is compatible with the culture and values of those affected, and maintains and strengthens community identity.
3. *Economic sustainability:* Development is economically efficient and resources are managed so they can support future generations.
4. *Local sustainability:* Development is designed to benefit local communities and sustain profits for local businesses.

Much of the thinking on sustainable tourism evolved from the preparations for, and results of, the historic Rio Earth Summit held in 1992, which developed the following framework:

- Travel & Tourism should assist people in leading healthy and productive lives in harmony with nature.
- Travel & Tourism should contribute to the conservation, protection and restoration of the earth's ecosystem
- Travel & Tourism should be based upon sustainable patterns of production and consumption
- Nations should cooperate to promote an open economic system, in which international trade in Travel & Tourism services can take place on a sustainable basis

- Travel & Tourism, peace, development and environmental protection are interdependent
- protectionism in trade in Travel & Tourism services should be halted or reversed
- environmental protection should constitute an integral part of the tourism development process
- tourism development issues should be handled with the participation of concerned citizens, with planning decisions being adopted at local level
- nations shall warn one another of natural disasters that could affect tourists or tourist areas.
- Travel & Tourism should use its capacity to create employment for women and indigenous peoples to the fullest extent
- tourism development should recognize and support the identity, culture, and interests of indigenous peoples
- international laws protecting the environment should be respected by the Travel & Tourism industry (World Travel and Tourism Council 1995, p. 1)

For sustainable tourism to be successful, the tourism industry, governments at all levels, key associations, and interested nonprofit organizations must endorse it. In 1992, the U.K. interest group Tourism Concern, in coordination with the World Wide Fund for Nature, published a discussion document titled "Beyond the Green Horizon: Principles for Sustainable Tourism," outlining the following principles, among others:

Using resources in a sustainable manner: The conservation of resources—natural, social, and cultural—is crucial and makes long-term business sense.

Reducing overconsumption and waste: Reduction of overconsumption and waste avoids the costs of putting right long-term environmental damage and contributes to the quality of tourism.

Maintaining diversity: Natural, social, and cultural diversity are essential for long-term sustainable tourism and create a resilient base for the industry.

Integrating tourism into planning: Integration into a national and local strategic planning framework and the use of environmental impact assessments increase the long-term viability of tourism.

Supporting local economies: Tourism that supports a wide range of local economic activities and takes environmental costs and values into account both protects those economies and avoids environmental damage.

Involving local communities: The full involvement of local communities in the tourism sector not only benefits them and the environment in general but also improves the quality of the tourism experience.

Consulting stakeholders and the public: Consultation between the tourism industry and local communities, organizations, and institutions is essential if they are to work together and resolve conflicts of interest.

Training staff: Staff training that integrates sustainable tourism into work practices, along with recruitment of local personnel at all levels, improves the quality of the tourism product.

Marketing tourism responsibly: Marketing that provides tourists with full and responsible information increases respect for the natural, social, and cultural environments of destination areas and enhances customer satisfaction.

Undertaking research: Ongoing research and monitoring by the industry using effective data collection and analysis tools is essential to solve problems and to bring benefits to destinations, the industry, and consumers.

Key to these broad principles, which underlie the action steps suggested later in this book, is the fact that managed sustainable tourism is often in companies' commercial interests and that responsibility for sustainable tourism is a shared public-private venture.

Numerous new sustainable tourism principles, concepts, and philosophies are developed each year. In 2002, for example, a multi-stakeholder consultation facilitated by the United Nations Environment Program produced an interesting report titled *Industry as a Partner for Sustainable Development* (World Travel and Tourism Council et al. 2002). Participants included the World Travel and Tourism Council, the International Federation of Tour Operators, the International Hotel and Restaurant Association, and the International Council of Cruise Lines. The report emphasizes the importance of management, education, and technology in improving opportunities for local populations, especially in rural areas. The following quotation summarizes many of the concepts developed in the report:

> The challenge is to move from the existing *ad hoc* approach, to one that can integrate the current social, economic, and environmental programs, funds, and initiatives, and evolve new patterns of managing travel and tourism businesses in a more systematic and dynamic way. The inevitable transition to sustainable development strategies gives the travel and tourism industry an opportunity to confirm itself as a solution, rather than a contributor to the economical, social, and environmental challenges facing the future. (p. 7)

One of the most active organizations in this area in the United States since 2001 has been Business Enterprises for Sustainable Travel (BEST), which subscribes to the highest principles of sustainable tourism development. BEST produces important case studies, hosts international conferences, and otherwise promotes the "best" in sustainable tourism management.

For sustainable tourism to be successful, long-term policies that balance environmental, social, and economic issues must be fashioned. Often it is the education of all the partners in tourism that will chart the future course of action. The case study at the end of this chapter illustrates how the Ecuadorian government has attempted to protect the Galapagos Islands from overdevelopment and overexposure. Considerably more work is needed to ensure a quality sustainable tourism future for the Galapagos, but progress is being made, and people are becoming better educated and more aware of the consequences if protective policies fail.

CASE STUDY: ECUADOR—THE WONDERFUL WORLD OF THE GALAPAGOS ISLANDS

Ecuador is ideally suited for a discussion of sustainable tourism. Its great varieties of topography and climate have contributed to the development of distinct landscapes and ecosystems. From the tropical rain forests that cover the Amazon region to the desert thickets of the coast, Ecuador is refuge to a diversity of species difficult to find anywhere else on earth.

Ecuador also has a rich history, diverse culture, and deeply rooted traditions, interesting buildings and fabricated attractions throughout the country, and ethnic festivals and local celebrations of interest to visitors. In brief, Ecuador has tremendous tourism potential.

The government of Ecuador recognized many years ago the importance of conserving its rich natural legacy. This consciousness, in concert with the growing worldwide environmental movement, led the government to take steps to see that specific tourist and ecological areas were preserved and protected so that future generations could continue to enjoy the country's abundant natural life. The approach to preservation has been largely through the development of national parks, a sustainable tourism development policy that promotes conservation and ensures ecological balance as tourism increases. Much of the maintenance and development of the parks is financed by fees charged to tourists.

Although Ecuador has numerous national parks, one park can be used to illustrate the need for continuous attention to sustainable tourism development: the world famous Galapagos Islands, which account for approximately 60 percent of the income that the Ecuadorian government receives from tourism.

The Galapagos Islands, officially named the Archipiélago de Colon in 1892 to commemorate the 400th anniversary of Christopher Columbus's discovery of America, are located in the Pacific Ocean, approximately 1,000 kilometers (600 miles) from the Ecuadorian coast, straddling the equator. The archipelago consists of thirteen major islands and numerous small islands of volcanic origin, of which 95 percent of the land is designated as a national park. The archipelago is known worldwide for its many unusual species of flora and fauna, which make it a living laboratory for studying the phenomenon of evolution. In 1835 Charles Darwin visited the islands while sailing on *HMS Beagle* as a geologist. His interest in the biology and geology of the islands led to several publications, books, and scientific papers recording the observations that served as the basis for his ideas regarding *The Origin of Species* (a controversial treatise on evolution that Darwin took almost twenty-five years to complete). Since Darwin's famous voyage, the marine and terrestrial ecosystems of the

Galapagos Islands have provided a wealth of information and a source of special environmental interests.

Many species are unique to the islands. Among the most outstanding are the Galapagos turtles, iguanas (both land and marine), sea lions, fur seals, blue-footed boobies, and finches. The Galapagos National Park is immensely popular with international tourists and is of major economic significance in terms of international tourism trade receipts for Ecuador. Tourism has benefited the islands and the country of Ecuador.

A book by William Beebe, *Galápagos: World's End,* published in 1924, led to the arrival of international travelers and the beginnings of ecotourism as it exists today on the Galapagos Islands. U.S. President Franklin D. Roosevelt was one of the early tourists to the islands in 1938. A few such early tourists remained and began businesses, enjoying the simple lifestyle. The real influx of tourism and its resulting economic benefits began in 1970 with approximately 1,000 visitors, and tourism has increased significantly since then, providing an important source of foreign exchange and employment. Because of their uniqueness and special significance internationally, the Galapagos Islands have been designated a World Heritage Site.

In 1935, the government of Ecuador set aside most of the islands in the Galapagos as a wildlife sanctuary to commemorate the 100th anniversary of Darwin's visit. The uninhabited areas were declared a national park in 1959. In 1964, the Charles Darwin Research Station began operating with initial support from the World Wildlife Fund. In 1968, Ecuador established the boundaries of the park, which includes 95 percent of the islands' land. Later, 54,000 square miles of ocean surrounding the islands was declared a marine reserve. Of the world's greatest marine reserves, only Australia's Great Barrier Reef is larger.

A key policy question for the Galapagos National Park is attaining a proper balance of visitors and family settlements without destroying the natural habitat. Families have settled there in search of a better standard of living as salaries on the islands are approximately 75 percent higher than in the rest of Ecuador. Uncontrolled growth of tourism to the islands, however, will threaten the quality of the visitor experience, the economic viability of the industry, and the ecological integrity of the islands themselves. It is a classic case of a popular site producing large visitor demand, and thus potentially generating large revenues, but in an area of fragile ecosystems that cannot endure heavy disturbances. The annual number of visitors is carefully monitored, and the National Park Service has published a set of behavioral guidelines for all visitors, best summed up by the instructions "Take only pictures. Leave only your footprints."

In 1974, the original management plan for the Galapagos National Park called for an annual maximum of 12,000 visitors; however, in 1978 that number was increased to 25,000, with the caveat that all activities on the islands should be performed under strict control. The actual number of visitors increased from 7,500 in 1975 to 32,595 in 1987, and many researchers are now concerned that this excessive and uncontrolled flow may be causing severe environmental degradation. The Ecuadorian government is studying this question carefully to find an appropriate answer. It has issued special "Galapagos National Park Rules" to help travelers realize the importance of protecting the park. For example, no one can go ashore in Galapagos unless accompanied by a licensed guide who is responsible for no more than sixteen visitors at a time. On the small ships operating in Galapagos, tourists must stay together with the one guide on board. On the larger ships, tourists are assigned to one guide for the trip's duration. Although great progress has been made in trying to preserve the islands for future generations, it is a constant battle to balance the visitors, local community, and the natural habitat.

Chapter 3

Is Sustainable Tourism Economically Viable?

A growing number of countries are recognizing that the world's appetite for experiencing environments and culture other than their own is a global economic opportunity.

John Naisbitt, *Global Paradox,* 1994

THINKING THROUGH SUSTAINABLE TOURISM

The new millennium is seeing a worldwide increase in travel for millions of people in both developed and developing countries. Shorter working hours, greater individual prosperity, faster and cheaper travel, and advanced technology have all helped to make leisure and travel one of the fastest-growing industries in the world. Today, tourism is indeed an activity of considerable global economic importance. Its growing significance as a source of income and employment, and as a major factor in the balance of payments for many countries, has been attracting attention from governments, regional and local authorities, and others with an interest in economic development.

The opportunity that tourism offers for positive economic and social benefits for tomorrow will depend on the decisions made today. We can plan well for the development of tourism or let it happen haphazardly and hope for the best. If we do not define clear-cut policies and plans now, we may never get another chance. We have a limited environment to work with, and much of it is already under siege from many different industrial and technological developments. To preserve our resources and derive benefits for tourism is indeed a management challenge. Having understandable sustainable tourism policies will help chart a favorable course for tourism and ensure its positive future growth.

The policy question often raised is whether tourism can be economically viable for private companies and local communities while also being sensitive to environmental, cultural, and social needs and meeting the requirements of visitors. The short answer is yes. However, no easy policy can achieve these goals. A successful and well-developed tourism program should include sustainable tourism management that seeks to meet the economic, ecological, social, cultural, and security objectives of the local community.

Another concern is that sustainable tourism development cannot meet or will detract from policies aimed at economic growth. Sustainable tourism policy should not be thought of as antigrowth. In fact, in most circumstances, it is progrowth. It has the capacity to increase the quality and lifetime value of the tourism products and, hence, increase visitor satisfaction. Satisfied visitors are likely to be repeat visitors and, in the long run, are key to the overall economic growth of tourism for a local community. The more important question is whether governments, private sector entities, local communities, nonprofit organizations, and tourists are ready to accept, plan for, participate in, lobby for, and manage tourism programs that are environmentally, socially, culturally, and economically sensitive.

Local community efforts to expand tourism should, after conducting a tourism inventory and assessing the potential, develop a set of best practices guidelines for sustainable tourism development. Suggested approaches include

- developing a strategic marketing plan that includes the concept of sustainable tourism;
- developing local guidelines for well-managed tourism programs; and
- recognizing that sustainable tourism can provide a basis for long-term growth.

Marketing tourism products as "sustainable" benefits the local community while appealing to tourists. Through well-developed products, the visitor may get a better understanding of the history, heritage, culture, and arts of the destination. At the same time, the local population can take pride in the variety of the tourism products and in its own heritage and environmental and cultural values.

The second suggestion is that well-managed programs can help maintain and protect natural and artificial attractions while allowing wide access to the natural environment and different cultural heritages. Developing new sustainable tourism products, recognizing visitor-carrying capacities, and creating cooperative programs between the government and the private sector are ways in which a local community can better develop its tourism attractions to provide long-term opportunities.

In terms of the third suggestion, tourism businesses are beginning to recognize that a quality natural and built environment enhances their ability to expand the tourism product into the future. They understand that tourists are demanding more products with a strong environmental, heritage, and cultural content. Local tourism programs, therefore, need to form partnerships to market and promote the environmental protection policies that are in their best interests. In brief, both local residents and tourists have the right to live and travel in quality environments, and businesses have the right to earn economic benefits from marketing quality tourism environments.

THE ECONOMICS OF COMMUNITY GROWTH THROUGH TOURISM

Global numbers do not indicate trends in the economic benefits of tourism to local communities. Many studies examined the local economic, social, cultural, and environmental aspects of tourism, and the results are largely very positive. See, for example, *Stories Across America: Opportunities for Rural Tourism* (National Trust for Historic Preservation 2001b), "Experiences and Benefits: A Heritage Tourism Development Model" (Sem et al. 1997), and *Sustainable Tourism Development: A Guide for Local Planners* (World Tourism Organization 1993). Numerous case studies have also been conducted and published by Business Enterprises for Sustainable Tourism. However, a local community contemplating tourism as an economic development tool should begin with a comprehensive study. Tourism is not necessarily a panacea for economic woes. A careful cost-benefit analysis should be conducted as well as economic, environmental, and social impact studies. A key consideration in an overall evaluation of the impact of tourism is its ability to provide future benefits to the host community. In general, most studies have found that a well-researched, well-planned, and well-managed tourism program that takes into account the local, natural, and cultural environment has a good chance of improving the local economy and enhancing the quality of life of residents. The economic benefits include new businesses, job growth, increased income, new products, improved infrastructure, economic diversification, and economic integration of the local economy, and special opportunities to link with other services and products. Approached in the right way, tourism can also promote community pride.

Local economic benefits also include profitable domestic industries such as lodging, restaurants, transport systems, convention centers, entertainment, souvenirs, handicraft shops, and guide services. When local tourism attracts large numbers of international visitors it can generate sizable amounts of foreign exchange. Potential benefits to rural areas, in particular, where employment may be sporadic or insufficient, include a wider job base, capital investment, and new demand for agricultural produce.

A community's initial inventory and assessment of its historic sites and buildings, traditions, culture, heritage, attractions, and natural beauty might suggest preserving these assets for future generations and for long-term economic and social gain. The economic value in the protection of such assets is that it helps both small and large communities enhance their overall tourism potential. Recent studies have demonstrated that an increasing number of travelers are interested in seeing and doing more and are willing to stay longer and spend more money in areas that sustain the culture and environment.

STRATEGIC PLANNING FOR SUSTAINABLE TOURISM

A carefully designed strategy for sustainable tourism may offer a quality environment and improved living standards for future generations. Economic growth through tourism can be compatible with sustainable tourism development—in other words, with quality growth. Tourism development must clearly be participatory, involving local peoples and businesses in decisions that affect their lives. Reaching the goal of sustainable tourism development requires concomitant progress in at least five closely related dimensions: economic, human, environmental, political, and technological. Actions in one dimension can reinforce, expand, or enhance goals in another.

Sustainable tourism development may require some changes in existing policies and practices depending on each locale. Some of these changes may be major, but the results will make them worthwhile in the long run. Progress will depend on strong local, state/province, and national leadership in partnership with the continued commitment of people in local communities to a sustainable tourism strategy. Increasingly, this will include a growing body of private organizations interested in and dedicated to positively influencing the environment. Local participation and/or control are key to the success of sustainable tourism development.

Tourism based on environmental and cultural concerns should be embraced in any economic development process for a local community. Tourist attractions in both the natural and built environments, such as unspoiled natural ecosystems, well-maintained historic sites, and cultural heritage events, are tremendous engines for economic growth and can produce quality-of-life benefits.

The problem that governments and the private sector often have with defining the economics of protecting the environment is attempting to assign values to the protected resource. Some economic research is aimed at producing environmental indicators along the same lines as economic indicators (World Tourism Organization 2004). The key will be finding good management techniques to support sustainable tourism goals, though plenty of good strategic examples can be found already in the preservation of nature tourism sites. For example, the U.S. Fish and Wildlife Service provides numerous guide publications related to good wildlife management programs to help tourists enjoy their visits. Such efforts, plus others at the local level, will create a quality tourism product and increased opportunities for growth. Compiling the information and educating a broad spectrum of the public is what will ultimately provide the answers. One organization mentioned in Chapter 2, Business Enterprises for Sustainable Travel (BEST), is providing some of this education through case studies that highlight successful business practices in sustainable tourism. These case studies are used by travel and tourism companies to advance their business objectives while enhancing the social and economic well-being of destination communities. BEST's mission "is to create and disseminate knowledge for the travel and tourism industry and the traveling public on business practices that enrich destination communities, enhance travelers' experiences, and promote economic prosperity." BEST "identifies practices that contribute to the long-term sustainability of the communities in which the travel and tourism industry operates."[1]

MARKETING THE SUSTAINABLE TOURISM PRODUCT

Sustainable tourism, including ecotourism, adventure tourism, learning vacations, cultural tourism, and heritage tourism (to name a few), is definitely on the rise. For example, 40 to 60 percent of international tourists "travel to enjoy and appreciate nature." More important, such tourists take longer trips and spend more money. A more recent summary in the thirteenth annual edition of *Tourism Works for America* (Travel Industry Association of America 2004) states that sustainable tourism had been an aspect of more than half of the top ten activities of U.S. resident travelers in the previous year.

Some areas of the world have recognized the importance of sustainable tourism and, for the most part, are marketing its positive elements. The United States has made rapid strides in the new millennium but has a lot of catching up to do in terms of managing sustainable tourism. Both the public and private sectors at the national, state, and local levels in the United States already are striving to promote public respect of cultural, ecological, and historic tourism resources. At the national level, the U.S. National Park Service and the U.S. Heritage Conservation and Recreation Service focus public awareness on the need to conserve unique national treasures. In 1997, the U.S. Department of Agriculture's Forest Service commissioned an important study, "Experiences and Benefits: A Heritage Tourism Development Model," highlighting a systematic approach toward heritage tourism (Sem et al. 1997). The congressionally chartered National Trust for Historic Preservation, through its acquisition of historic properties, study tours, and other educational programs such as the "National Main Street Program," has demonstrated that preservation and development can work together to everyone's advantage. As mentioned in Chapter 2 and demonstrated in the case study in Chapter 7, North Carolina is one of the leading U.S. states with respect to sustainable tourism. Many of the state's governmental agencies and offices focus on efforts to support such tourism (the rural, heritage, cultural, and natural environments). Kansas, too, has recognized that sustainable tourism in many of the rural areas of the state may just be enough to "sustain" the economy for struggling communities.

Certainly such countries as Belize, Costa Rica, Dominica, Ecuador, and Jamaica have realized the value of sustainable tourism. For example, in 2005 Belize conducted marketing campaigns that focused on its natural environment, recognizing that managing its sustainable tourism products offers economic growth for the future. Some regional efforts are also underway; for example, the Eastern Caribbean States have started a "Preserving Paradise" project, described in a brochure as follows:

> Many of us and our visitors believe that the islands of the Caribbean are the closest thing to paradise. To help keep them that way, the governments of six countries of the Organization of Eastern Caribbean States, Antigua and Barbuda, Dominica, Grenada, St. Kitts and Nevis, St. Lucia and St. Vincent and the Grenadines, have set up an OECS Solid and Ship Generated Waste Management Project. It aims to reduce the amount of garbage generated in our homes and businesses, and improve the collection and disposal of such garbage in the OECS countries and of ship-generated solid waste. The project was conceived under the International Waters component of the Global Environment Facility that recognizes that the marine environment is heavily polluted with garbage, which threatens marine life as well as being unsightly when it washes up on the beaches of tourism dependent countries of the region. Though much of that garbage originates from ships, a large percentage is derived from land-based sources that border the Caribbean Sea. Garbage knows no boundaries. That's why a regional solution is necessary. In addition, the OECS is complying with 1973 International Convention for the Prevention of Pollution from Ships that sets specific recommendations for the disposal of ship-generated refuse. Across the island, locals will pay environmental levies or collection charges which will help to recover the cost of better service, while all air and sea visitors will pay a levy of US$1.50, starting December 1, 1998. The payback from im-

proved waste management is an improvement in our own quality of life. A cleaner country means fewer health risks and less
money spent on garbage. Preserving our unspoiled beauty means
better prospects for our tourism industry. Through this Project,
we are cleaning up our environment, preserving paradise and
safeguarding our future.[2] (OECS, 2005: http://www.oceanatlas
.com/unatlas/uses/uneptcxtsph/wastesph/2596carib.html)

Other areas of the world are rapidly beginning to market sustainable tourism products as that market niche increases in importance.
Australia, Canada, Costa Rica, Europe, and New Zealand have generally been ahead of the world curve in terms of effectively developing
and marketing sustainable tourism. The United Kingdom and France
have made outstanding progress in marketing their heritage and cultural sites. Parts of Asia and Africa are making some progress, as is
the Middle East. Jeju Island is South Korea's best representative of
sustainable tourism. Latin American countries, through the efforts of
the Organization of American States, are making strides to improve
their sustainable tourism products. Still, considerable work remains.

The market for new tourism products will become ever more competitive. For sustainable tourism, such competition will require even
greater cooperation at the local level among government, business interests, and nonprofit entities. In effect, competitive elements at the
local level will be bound together in cooperative arrangements. This
strategy of local *coop*eration in order to meet comp*etition* more effectively regionally, nationally, and internationally is sometimes referred to as "coopetition," a concept introduced to the tourism industry in 1995 by David L. Edgell Sr. and R. Todd Haenisch in their book
Coopetition: Global Tourism Beyond the Millennium. "Coopetition"
recognizes that businesses and local communities can form partnerships to become more competitive. It has numerous applications to
sustainable tourism as businesses compete to increase their profit-
ability but at the same time cooperate to protect and preserve the environment. It is a proactive approach that fits the creative strategies
needed in the area of sustainable tourism management.

Sustainable tourism has also had to look at the economic impact of
marketing old products in new ways. A recent example that comes to
mind is the marketing of certain safaris in Kenya and Tanzania. Although tourist safaris are a very old proposition, many new approaches are careful to take into account the need to impact as little as

possible on the flora and fauna of the safari area. At the same time, the economic value of the safari helps to preserve the product. Finding a balance or the "carrying capacity" of an area becomes critical. If we look at the safari in the broadest terms, it just very well may be that tourism will save certain animals from extinction. If the local community benefits in terms of jobs and income from safaris, it will be more likely to unite with the government to prevent poaching, put aside land for parks and preserves, and otherwise help protect the flora and fauna of the area. If an animal is worth $5,000 to the poacher, but $50,000 to be seen by many tourists, people have a strong incentive to preserve the animal and its habitat and to prevent poaching. This simplified example can be generalized, but each element of such a process must be analyzed so that the greater benefits of sustainable tourism are magnified many times over before a decision is made.

Big Cedar Lodge and its additions, Dogwood Canyon Nature Park and Top of the Rock golf course, included as the case study in this chapter, are examples of the best attributes of resort development compatible with the precepts of sustainable tourism. Big Cedar Lodge is also a good example of coopetition in its partnership with the nearby popular destination of Branson, Missouri, which hosted approximately 7 million visitors in 2004. (Although these two destinations have quite different tourism products, their cooperative marketing approach makes them more effective in surpassing their competition.) This very popular and highly profitable resort answers part of the policy question raised at the beginning of this chapter: "Can tourism be economically viable for private companies and local communities while also being sensitive to environmental, cultural, and social needs?" Big Cedar Lodge demonstrates that with a forward-looking view, creative thinking, and innovative marketing, sustainable tourism can add appreciably to economic growth.

CASE STUDY: MISSOURI, BIG CEDAR LODGE—
THE EPITOME OF SUSTAINABLE TOURISM

Big Cedar Lodge, near Branson, Missouri, is a wilderness resort that offers rustic outdoor activities. It rests in the heart of Ozark Mountain country, a region distinctively characterized by rugged remoteness, natural beauty, diverse features, and rich history. The resort respects the sanctity of nature and fosters most of the concepts of sustainable tourism development and management presented in this book. It looms over a body of water, Table Rock Lake, with 43,000 acres of clear blue-green expanses, yet surrenders to neighboring woods. The lodge is a tribute to man's ability to blend built structures with a strong presence of their own into a natural setting.

The area is rich in Native American heritage and culture, both ancient and more recent. In the 1800s these were the hunting grounds of the Osage Indians, and before the influx of white trappers and explorers, the Osage lived in harmony with the natural habitat, which has an abundance of flora and fauna. Fortunately, the present owner of the resort understands the importance of the history of the area and is a conservationist who also advocates sustainable tourism development. It is a place of adventure and excitement that strives to maintain a positive sustainable development ecosystem.

The guiding philosophy behind the continued development of Big Cedar Lodge is the idea that the principal asset of the project is its wilderness setting. It is important that the natural habitat, which is an integral part of Big Cedar Lodge, is not a victim of tourism and development, but rather a beneficiary. In this regard, the preservation of plants and wildlife is of primary concern. Every effort is made to accommodate animals relocated from cleared areas, utilities are located underground, the integrity of natural waterways is maintained, new plant life is introduced appropriately, and the buildings are designed to respect the environment and cultural heritage of the existing community.

In the early 1920s, two wealthy Missouri friends—Julian "Jude" Simmons, a manufacturing and real estate entrepreneur, and Harry L. Worman, a retired Frisco railroad president—decided to build themselves backcountry resort homes in the Ozarks. Together, they bought 300 acres of oak forest and cedar glade along the Long Creek Branch of White River in Big Cedar Hollow, now the site of Big Cedar Lodge. Jude Simmons built his log mansion in Big Cedar Hollow as a sportsman's vacation retreat, patterning it after the grand wilderness architecture that the northeastern elite favored for their Adirondack resorts. Harry Worman built a Tudor-style stone and stucco home, caretaker's cottage, and garage overlooking the scenic Big Cedar Valley. When Worman was in his mid-sixties, he married an eighteen-year-old beauty, Dorothy, from Springfield, Missouri. As a wedding gift to his religious wife he added a small chapel with stained-glass windows to their house. A real estate man and hotel operator, Dan Norris, purchased the tract in 1947. Norris added a hotel lodge and a swimming pool, and, with twenty-five horses, opened a resort he called Devil's Pool Guest Ranch.

The White River was dammed in 1954 to form Table Rock Lake, a sprawling 43,000-acre reservoir whose clear waters serve as Big Cedar Lodge's natural boundary. When Bass Pro Shops bought the property in 1987, founder John L. Morris proceeded with care to restore the Worman and Simmons buildings to their original magnificence. He also renovated the lodges in authentic rustic Adirondack tradition. As an active and dedicated conservationist, he rejuvenated the natural beauty of Big Cedar Hollow.

The Big Cedar Lodge area was augmented in 1990 when Morris purchased 2,230 acres to expand the natural environmental area. Shortly thereafter he increased this to a total of nearly 10,000 acres to develop a private wilderness refuge, the Dogwood Canyon Nature Park. This park, twenty minutes from Big Cedar Lodge, is a special commitment to the preservation of nature.

Dogwood Canyon Nature Park, which opened for guest tours in 1996, is an unspoiled expanse of bowed ridges and deep hollows covered in oak pine and cedar. The sheer limestone bluffs are honeycombed with numerous caves. Archeologists have unearthed Indian burials, artifacts, and ancient cliff-dwelling remains. Herds of buffalo, Texas longhorn cattle, and elk make Dogwood Canyon their home.

In 1997, Big Cedar Lodge added a "naturalist" Top of the Rock golf course. The golf course, like Big Cedar Lodge and Dogwood Canyon Nature Park, was built in wilderness splendor, preserving the pristine beauty of the area. It is the first Jack Nicklaus signature par 3 nine-hole course ever built, and because of its commitment to the environment and the inhabitants, has been recognized as an Audubon Signature Course by Audubon International, making it one of only six courses in the country in 1997 with that distinction.

Today, Big Cedar Lodge is a model of what can be accomplished successfully and profitably if the principles of sustainable tourism development are adhered to. People want to visit the lodge's pleasant natural surroundings, enjoy its many outdoor activities, learn about its rich heritage and history, and marvel at the magnificence of this unique rural tourism area. It is sustainable tourism at its finest. The challenge for Big Cedar Lodge and similar properties is whether future managers will continue to be enlightened and supportive of sustainable tourism.

Chapter 4

Nature-Based Tourism:
Don't Fool with Mother Nature

To the body and mind which have been cramped by noxious
work or company, nature is medicinal and restores their tone.

Ralph Waldo Emerson

NATURE-BASED TOURISM WAS NEVER SO GOOD

The principal components of sustainable tourism include tourism
in the natural environment (often referred to as "ecotourism"), heritage (locations), culture (sites), and rural areas. The natural environment component is what many travelers are seeking—an odyssey full
of water, vegetation, archaeological and cultural sites, historic and
heritage monuments, and the simple beauty of the countryside. The
flora and fauna of the natural habitat may attract a large segment of
visitors. Sometimes the attraction is the historical, military, or religious context and traditions, or it may be the high level of preservation, integrity, and homogeneity of an area— the rich heritage of a
place—that makes it an exciting tourism destination. A cultural activity or the desire to gain a better understanding of how others live on
the planet may appeal to many tourists. Alternatively, rural tourism,
which encompasses "agritourism," brings many visitors to certain areas. In a holistic approach, these various parts are intertwined into the
composite "sustainable tourism." For purposes of clarification and insight, it is useful to review some of the pieces separately before
collectively combining them to determine positive ways to manage
sustainable tourism.

It is often the natural environment that attracts the tourist in the
first place. Pleasant climates, scenic wonders, beautiful coastlines

41

and beaches, majestic mountains and valleys, rugged woods interspersed with rolling plains, magnificent skylines, and the rhythmic sounds of the sea are among the natural attractions that cause large movements of people worldwide. For others, it is the opportunity for an unobstructed view of the light of the rising sun, the serene glow of the moon, the intensity of the stars, and the endless diversity of natural resources that add to the value of travel and the quality of life of the traveler and the resident alike. Key to successful environmental tourism is balancing the number of visitors with the capacities of a given environment in a way that allows for the greatest interaction with the least disruption and destruction. In other words, the question is whether we can enjoy nature and at the same time leave it relatively unspoiled. Opinions differ on how this can best be accomplished; however, most would agree that the management of natural resources is a good beginning point.

The United Nations designated 2002 the year of "ecotourism"; according to its views on the natural environment, as reported in *The Environmental Magazine* (Montavalli 2002) ecotourism must include the following elements:

- Its main motivation is "the observation and appreciation of nature as well as the traditional cultures prevailing in natural areas."
- It contains "educational and interpretation features."
- It is organized "for small groups by specialized and small, locally owned businesses."
- It minimizes negative impacts "upon the natural and sociocultural environment."
- It supports the protection of natural areas by
  1. generating income for host communities;
  2. providing alternative employment and income opportunities;
  3. increasing awareness of the need for conservation of natural and cultural assets.[1]

As these recommendations become better known, communities are becoming better educated to understand them and developers are increasingly interested in incorporating them into projects. Others engaged in natural environmental tourism, or ecotourism, would likely agree with these elements but might add other attributes noted in Chapters 8, 9, and 10.

History suggests that tourists and the environment are not always very compatible. Some tourists want such souvenirs as special corals, exotic rocks, or seashells. Others trample irreplaceable tundra or otherwise alter natural flora and fauna. Examples abound of the problem of not maintaining a proper balance between tourism and the environment. The case study on the Galapagos Islands illustrates the issues that arise from many years of overvisitation. The Ecuadorian government recognized that too many people lived on or traveled to this fragile environment and is seeking to balance the economic benefits for the islands' inhabitants with the need to protect the environment so that future generations can also enjoy this very special destination.

Worldwide, dirty beaches are a problem to be addressed by the tourism industry—particularly in many Caribbean destinations, where debris left behind by residents and tourists has a negative impact on the beauty of the islands. Alongside the actual and potential impact of petroleum spills is the impact of the garbage that cruise lines sometimes dump into the sea, not only polluting the water, but also leading to befouling of the beaches along the sea routes. Recently, the Caribbean has come to grips with this problem and is addressing it as a region.

People and institutions are realizing the need to protect the very pristine environment that provided the tourist attraction in the first place. Yellowstone National Park, for instance, has taken important steps to balance visitation and preservation. The U.S. National Park Service continually reviews and revises its policies to protect fragile areas so that new generations of visitors have an opportunity to see the wonderful national park treasures. The National Park System Advisory Board Report (2001), *Rethinking the National Parks for the 21st Century,* includes as one of its recommendations the need to "[a]dvance the principles of sustainability, while first practicing what is preached." In other words, good resource and people management in the parks is the key to sustaining tourism opportunities for future generations. The challenge in managing sustainable tourism over the next few years will be to impart through the natural environment a quality-of-life dimension to the tourism experience. This will not happen spontaneously; it will have to become an integral part of the policy and planning process for tourism development.

Properly organized and managed tourism can provide an incentive for the protection of national parks, the enhancement of certain environmental areas, and the education of the traveling public. In many places, tourist expenditures provide the funds to protect the environment. Thus, to some degree, it is high-paying safari-bound tourists who are providing the economic means to save lions, gorillas, and cheetahs in Africa from extinction (and from poachers).

We can find good examples worldwide of tourism development compatible with the environment, including the Caneel Bay Resort in St. John, U.S. Virgin Islands, which is designed to accommodate tourists very comfortably without encroaching on or altering the natural surroundings. The resort has a clear policy designed to protect the environment that is explained to the guests and includes guidelines for the interaction of tourists with the island's natural resources. Similarly, the 1,040-acre Ventana Canyon resort community in Arizona has been deliberately designed to be sensitive to the local environment, and another Arizona resort development, The Boulders, has been built to blend with the surrounding area and with the natural habitat. A new Hyatt Regency development near Scottsdale, Arizona, is confined to 27 acres of the 640 available acres in order to preserve the surrounding area, which is carefully maintained to protect the plant life and wildlife. And in Hawaii, where many environmental mistakes were made in the Waikiki area, a clear policy has emerged to avoid similar development in the future. For example, the Mauna Lani Resort at Kalahuipuaa in West Hawaii took every care to enhance rather than obliterate the environment. The technology to develop resorts compatible with the environment is evolving rapidly, and it is up to tourism policymakers and planners and local communities to make sure such technology is properly utilized.

YES, TOURISM IMPACTS NATURAL AREAS

The Commission for Environmental Cooperation (CEC) located in Montreal, Canada, which includes Canada, Mexico, and the United States (under the aegis of the North American Free Trade Agreement), prepared a discussion paper in 1999 titled "The Development of Sustainable Tourism in Natural Areas in North America: Background, Issues and Opportunities." This document suggests that sustainable tourism in natural areas is an opportunity for the three countries to explore cooperation and "perhaps even a common framework, for the promotion of sustainable development through nature-based tourism. Underlying the economic benefits of development is a joint commitment to the protection of the ecosystems that attract tourists to natural areas" (Commission for Environmental Cooperation 1999). The paper's "Definitions and Context" (p. 7) include the following:

- Sustainable tourism is defined, in theoretical terms, as tourism development with minimal negative impacts and maximal positive impacts on the sociocultural and ecological environment through planning and management.
- Ecotourism, or sustainable tourism to natural areas, is a niche market. Numerous definitions of ecotourism are attempting to translate theory into practice.
- Different working definitions of the term "ecotourism" prevail both within and among Canada, Mexico, and the United States.
- Surveys of ecotourist profiles in Latin America, Canada, and the United States found that the average ecotourist tends to be older, with a graduate degree, a high level of disposable income, and an enjoyment of traveling with family or friends.
- Accurate data on ecotourism are difficult to obtain because of the varying definitions of the term, non-site-specific census methods, and a lack of relevant studies.
- Trends indicate that conventional tourism has grown over the past decade and continues to grow. They suggest a diversification and increase of tourism into alternative and specialized activities such as ecotourism, bird-watching, hiking, canoeing, and visiting natural settings and interesting cultures.
- Key North American natural and cultural tourism assets include ecological regions and landscapes, fauna and flora, protected spaces and species, cultural populations, sites, and artifacts.
- Participation by the local community is key to the long-term viability of tourism.
- History has proven that unplanned, unmanaged tourism that exceeds the carrying capacity of an area is transformed from a nonconsumptive renewable resource venture into a short-term "boom and bust" enterprise.
- Promoters of tourism and promoters of nature conservation are bound by three types of relationship: conflict, coexistence, or symbiosis. A symbiotic relationship from which both benefit is the ultimate goal.

In 2003, the CEC met in Washington, DC, to further discuss issues and concerns in sustainability related to the three countries.[2]

Sometimes when governments become involved in issues such as sustainable tourism, agreements to action may hinge on differences in definitions, cultural understandings, or linguistic interpretations. This is also true of relationships between private sector groups and local and national governments. However, Business Enterprises for Sustainable Travel (n.d.) has published a case study on one of the most progressive ecotravel companies in the world, Lindblad Expeditions, which has developed a highly successful model approach to ecotourism in the Galapagos Islands. Behind the company's success are its positive overarching sustainable tourism policies:

- Preserve a destination's natural assets to ensure its ongoing value to the travel industry and the local community
- Maintain positive relations with local government officials who determine business regulations
- Attract and retain employees who possess key skills
- Build and expand a loyal customer base

PROTECTING THE ENVIRONMENT THROUGH TOURISM DEVELOPMENT

A good example of protecting the environment through careful tourism development can be found in Queen Anne's County on the Maryland side of the Chesapeake Bay, an area rich in American history and heritage. Long before European settlers began to arrive in the 1600s, this was the home of several Native American tribes. The water and vegetation systems yielded rich plant and animal life that allowed the local residents to sustain life with comparative ease. The early settlers, too, found the area rich in productive land, the woods full of animal life, and the rivers and bay area a natural habitat for fish and fowl. Rapid development around 2002 meant that some of the charm of the rural environment began to disappear. However, some planners and tourism advisers recognized this trend and began to plan for sustainable tourism development.

The following excerpts are taken (with permission) from the 2002 publication "Natural Advantage" by I. Katherine Magruder, Director of Queen Anne's County Department of Business and Tourism in the

State of Maryland. This special report investigates "opportunities associated with developing, managing and promoting access to the wealth of natural environmental attractions indigenous to the County and surrounding region, and subsequently creating a strategy to proceed." In Magruder's words, "Sustaining the balance of community, economy and environment is our challenge. We believe this plan provides good direction and a method by which that goal may be achieved."

Several key reasons lie behind the choice of this particular area, illustrating some important points in the development of sustainable (eco)tourism. First, the county has developed a quality tourism product—a must before developing a marketing strategy. Also, as has been stressed in this book, the community must endorse and support the tourism effort, which it has done. The business sector in this case has worked closely with the community. The plan also stresses the supply side of tourism, that is, making sure that the service infrastructure is in place. Finally, the area's proximity to Washington, DC, gives it a natural market. All these ingredients combined offer a great opportunity for the county to develop and market its ecotourism product further, as is indicated in the plan. These are the highlights from the "Executive Summary" of the plan indicating the advantages enjoyed by the tourism industry in Queen Anne's County:

- The County's geographic location on the Chesapeake Bay and its associated rivers, wetlands, and uplands
- The County's position within the Atlantic Flyway, host to many thousands of migratory birds, not only waterfowl but also shorebirds, neotropical migrants, and raptors
- The relatively level terrain of the region and its small population, allowing easy bicycling on quiet country roads
- The beautiful countryside and well-tended communities (and historic sites), highly attractive to many Americans who enjoy driving for pleasure
- A concentration of important natural sites, including not only magnificent state and federal areas and parks, but also a strong nonprofit sector, devoted to preserving unique sites within the region. The non-profit sector is especially well equipped to provide high-quality environmental education programs to build public understanding of the region's unique environment

- A maritime tradition with Chesapeake Bay watermen and a strong seafood industry. There are many ways for visitors to gain access to the water or otherwise enjoy the flavor of a maritime community
- A community that has supported years of investment in outdoor recreation and the preservation of important habitat, ranging from the County's strong park system to its recent participation in the Rural Legacy Program
- A community that understands the importance of tourism to its economy and has supported significant investments in County programs and facilities (most recently the excellent Chesapeake Exploration Center) and in the planning necessary to take advantage of key state and federal programs for heritage areas and scenic byways
- A strong business sector devoted to friendly hospitality, from outfitting to accommodations needed by visitors seeking to enjoy the region. Queen Anne's County is among the Eastern Shore counties best positioned to provide the visitor services needed to support this Ecotourism Initiative

Trends in ecotourism, adventure, recreation, and heritage tourism and general visitor interest in the Chesapeake Bay region mean that Queen Anne's County has the opportunity to attract a growing number of desirable travelers. Initiatives to attract these visitors can result in significant private and public revenues. Accordingly, the Queen Anne's County Department of Business and Tourism has undertaken this ecotourism development plan to enable the county to compete effectively in the new market for ecotourism and adventure recreation related to the Chesapeake Bay.

Nowhere else on the Eastern Shore are so many opportunities available so close to one another for visitors to enjoy the Chesapeake Bay and learn about its natural systems. This "critical mass" of sites can support an ecotourism initiative designed to expand the region's tourism on a year-round basis, taking ready advantage of the hospitality offerings within Queen Anne's County. The county has a well-developed tourism service infrastructure in place, close to a large metropolitan market. With improvements suggested in this plan to develop more attractions or improve those already in place, the county can make greater use of this infrastructure and gain a larger share of the visitation from its primary markets.

Ecotourism or nature tourism has been around for a considerable time. The history of tourism is replete with examples of tourists and tourism destination managers subscribing to the need to preserve an area. Early accounts by Native Americans of what today is commonly referred to as nature tourism greatly preceded the discovery of America by the Europeans. After these accounts, the first written records in the United States that acknowledged the significance of nature-based tourism were penned by the Englishman John Lawson, a well-educated socialite and eager advocate of travel and adventure (Lawson 1709/1967).

Lawson put together a small band of adventurers consisting of Englishmen and Native American guides to travel and explore "Carolina" (now North and South Carolina). On December 28, 1700, the group departed Charles Town (now Charleston, South Carolina), traveling along the Santee River. Lawson kept a journal during this first expedition and made notes about each new plant and animal that he came across. He observed the differences of the land, the flora and fauna, and the Native American cultures; he recorded historical information provided by the inhabitants he visited and drew maps of the area. On this first trip he traveled some 550 miles in 59 days from Charles Town to what is known today as Bath, North Carolina. At that point some of the party left to explore other areas. Lawson built a house on high ground near a creek, still known as Lawson Creek near present-day New Bern, North Carolina. He then set about traveling throughout eastern North Carolina and beyond, including what is now the state of Virginia. In 1709 he published a book with the title page *A New Voyage to Carolina; Containing the Exact Description and Natural History of that Country: Together with the Present State thereof. And A Journal of a Thousand Miles, Travel'd thro' Several Nations of Indians. Giving a Particular Account of Their Customs, Manners, &c.* The book was quite popular in Europe and spurred a number of other adventurers of the time to travel to the New World. In 1711, traveling up the Neuse River with a friend, he was captured by the Tuscarora Indian tribe. His friend was released but Lawson was killed not too far from what is now Greenville, North Carolina. His notes, articles, and book stand as exemplars of early writings about nature-based travel. Although others were exploring the New World, no one understood what we today call ecotourism better than John Lawson or left such a substantial account of the nature, heritage, and culture of the time. The key today is finding a way that tourists and communities alike can enjoy quality nature-based tourism.

THE NAME OF THE GAME IS QUALITY

A quality step toward protecting the natural environment is the development by the American Society of Travel Agents (ASTA) of "The Ten Commandments of Ecotourism":

1. Respect the frailty of the earth. Realize that unless we are all willing to help in its preservation, unique and beautiful destinations may not be here for future generations to enjoy.
2. Leave only footprints—Take only photographs. No graffiti! No litter! Do not take away "souvenirs" from historical sites and natural sites.
3. To make your travels more meaningful, educate yourself about the geography, customs, manners and cultures of the regions you visit. Take time to listen to the people. Encourage local conservation efforts.
4. Respect the privacy and dignity of others. Inquire before photographing people.
5. Do not buy products made from endangered plants or animals, such as ivory, tortoise shell, animal skin and feathers. Read "Know Before You Go," the U.S. Customs list of products that cannot be imported.
6. Always follow designated trails. Do not disturb animals, plants or their natural habitats.
7. Learn about and support conservation-oriented programs and organizations working to preserve the environment.
8. Whenever possible, walk or utilize environmentally sound methods of transportation. Encourage drivers of public vehicles to stop engines when parked.
9. Patronize hotels, airlines, resorts, cruise lines, tour operators and suppliers that advance energy and environmental conservation; water and air quality; recycling; safe management of waste and toxic materials; noise abatement; community involvement; and that provide experienced, well-trained staff dedicated to strong principles of conservation.

10. Ask your ASTA travel agent to identify organizations that subscribe to ASTA Environmental Guidelines for air, land and sea travel. ASTA has recommended that these organizations adopt their own environmental codes to cover special sites and ecosystems.

These ten commandments have wide application beyond the clientele of ASTA, and the approach demonstrates what a concerned association can accomplish in supporting positive ecotourism.

The tourism industry, and most evidently nature-based tourism, cannot exist without a healthy environment. Sustainable management of natural resources is being recognized as leading to acceptable conservation and development of a higher-quality tourism product. Improving the quality of the tourism product is the best way to ensure the future growth of the industry.

It can be helpful to develop guidelines or codes of conduct similar to the examples in this chapter, as in the case of the Galapagos Islands. This approach has also been adopted for arctic tourism to limit the impacts on the natural environment and local communities of great numbers of visitors arriving at the same time on large ships.

Sensitivity to the environment is rapidly becoming a major component of international tourism marketing strategies; too often we see incidents where visitors are insensitive to their surroundings, which can ruin their welcome in a particular region and ultimately damage the industry as a whole. The important message, as stated previously, is that whatever the environment may be, it must be nurtured, managed, and promoted in ways that future generations can enjoy.

Tourism businesses today are recognizing that managing a quality environment enhances their ability to develop and promote tourism products now and into the future. Many understand that tourists are increasingly demanding products with a strong environmental content. By forming partnerships with local entities and heeding environmental protection policies, they can create and market quality tourism products.

Even very remote rural areas are finding ways to benefit from tourism and, at the same time, practice many of the precepts for sustainable tourism advocated in this book. The following case study, from a remote area of Panama, is a good illustration of what can be accomplished. The approach is very interesting.

CASE STUDY: SUSTAINABLE ECOTOURISM DEVELOPMENT IN THE EMBERÁ INDIGENOUS COMMUNITIES—CHAGRES NATIONAL PARK, PANAMA

The Emberá is one of seven indigenous tribes found in the Republic of Panama.[3] Historically this tribe comes from the Darien province in southeastern Panama on the border with Colombia, but as a result of political persecution and security concerns, some of the tribal members began immigrating into other provinces of Panama more than twenty-five years ago. Small Emberá communities were established along the banks of the Chagres River, the primary source of water for the Panama Canal. Here the Emberá practiced traditional subsistence agriculture and hunting and fishing, moving village locations from time to time to find better farming land or hunting and fishing areas. In 1984 the Chagres National Park was established, encompassing the area where the Emberá lived. Park regulations put restrictions on agriculture and cultural practices, greatly limiting the Emberá's source of income and their livelihood. The Emberá of the Chagres River were faced with finding a way to survive. Would they have to return to their homeland and face the same concerns that prompted their ancestors to leave? Most of the community members had been born and raised along the banks of the Chagres; it was their homeland.

The Emberá worked together to form a not-for-profit sustainable tourism organization and a community development organization. Today, they have curtailed their subsistence agriculture practices, which can be destructive to the rain forest. Working with the Panamanian Tourism Bureau, the Panamanian government's National Environmental Authority, local nongovernmental development organizations, and international conservation organizations, they are developing a Chagres River Basin Development Plan. They are hosting local and international tourists by interpreting their culture and the tropical rain forest in which they live, and they are enhancing their communities by improving drinking water, schools, and training for community members.

The Chagres National Park was legally established on October 2, 1984. It is one of the largest national parks in Panama, covering an area of approximately 130,000 hectares. It contains four life zones (very humid tropical, humid tropical, premontane humid, and premontane rain) and provides habitats for an enormous diversity of plant and wildlife species (many of which are endangered), including more than 500 bird species. The Chagres National Park contains the largest expanse of tropical forest in the Panama Canal watershed. Its rivers are the primary source of fresh water for the Panama Canal and the heavily populated urban areas of Panama City and Colon. The park is mostly remote and without roads, with spectacular wild and scenic areas.

Many small villages and human settlements are found within the park boundaries and in the buffer area around the park, where farmers scratch out a subsistence living. Although subsistence land use is often not compatible with park goals, most of the settlements existed before the park was created, making it difficult to relocate them to other areas.

The park is under the management of the Panamanian government's National Environmental Authority (Autoridad Nacional del Ambiente, known by its Spanish acronym ANAM). Its primary conservation goals are (1) to protect the watersheds that provide fresh water to the Panama Canal and Panama's major populated areas, (2) to protect the rich animal and plant biodiversity, and (3) to provide outdoor recreation for local and international tourists.

ANAM maintains several guard stations within the national park, but it lacks the human and financial resources needed for long-term sustainability. ANAM is interested in developing comanagement agreements with local communities and NGOs, as well as international NGOs, to assist with certain aspects of park management. Technical and financial assistance have come from foreign donors such as the U.S. Agency for International Development (USAID), the U.S. Forest Service, the German aid agency Deutsche Gesellschaft für Technische Zusammenarbeit (GTZ), and international NGOs such as The Nature Conservancy and Conservation International.

Four indigenous Emberá villages, with a combined population of approximately 330 people, have been established in the interior of the Chagres National Park—the first in 1975, several years before the creation of the park. Each village has traditional-style thatched-roof homes and a community center. Some have schools, elementary potable water systems, and small generator-operated electrical system. Each village is independent and self-governing, but the villages communicate with one another and work together when necessary.

In the late 1990s the Emberá began working closely with the Panamanian Institute of Tourism, ANAM, and local NGOs to develop a sustainable tourism plan for the Emberá villages of the Chagres River. The goal is to get the villages to work together and with governmental agencies, local tourism operators, and local NGOs to define viable long-term alternatives to their traditional subsistence agriculture way of life. The plan attempts to provide guidelines and direction for coordinated, sustainable tourism development in the Chagres River Basin. It outlines the current situation and the obstacles that will be faced by the Emberá in the development process, and it lays out a strategy of how best to provide high-quality tourism that coincides with environmental protection, conservation, and enhancement of the Emberá culture. The sustainable tourism plan is dynamic. It will be reviewed, updated, and altered constantly as the local situation changes and as tourism in the area matures.

The Emberá Drua community, one of the four indigenous communities in the area, started its tourism and community development project in 1996 with the formation of a community committee. Since 1996 the project has grown and evolved, and it is now being managed more as a small business. Today, the community has formed two NGOs, one for tourism (Tranchichi Emberá Chagres) and one for community development (Wanamera Emberama Chagres). Each NGO has a board of directors and objectives. In addition to learning tourism techniques, the Emberá are learning small-business practices (such as accounting, marketing, and planning) so that they can manage their NGOs in a more efficient and effective manner.

The NGOs have received training from the government of Panama's Authority for Micro-, Small, and Medium-Sized Businesses (AMPYME) in better business practices and assistance in legally registering their tourism project as a community-based microbusiness. A local NGO, the Association for the Development of Tourism (AFOTUR), is also providing technical assistance, guidance, and networking contacts to the Emberá NGOs. Through coordination with AFOTUR, the Emberá have received technical assistance from USAID, the U.S. Forest Service, and other international donors.

The Emberá Drua community offers "cultural ecotourism." The cultural aspect comes from the opportunity for the visitor to observe the traditional way of life and interact with the community members. The eco aspect relates to the opportunity to observe and experience nature in the heart of the Chagres National Park rain forest. All tourism is low impact to the environment and the Emberá culture. The Emberá practice a "carry it in, carry it out" policy, which means that tourists leave nothing behind.

Clients include lócal visitors (student groups and the general public) as well as international tourists (mostly passengers from cruise ships stopping in Panama). From January to May 2002, the Emberá Drua had an estimated 2,536 visitors, mostly from the United States and Panama. Activities on offer to the tourists include interpretation of the Emberá culture and way of life through storytelling, short talks, and dance, hiking and bird-watching on interpretive trails, swimming in the Chagres River, body painting with native plant dyes, meals of local food, traditional fishing in the Chagres River, and demonstrations of basket making and wood carving.

As with any project, there can and will be both positive and negative impacts. If the project is to be successful, the positive impacts must outweigh the negative ones, ideally by a wide margin. In 2002, Jerry Wylie and Gerald P. Bauer of the U.S. Forest Service worked with the Emberá Drua village to review its sustainable tourism program and make recommendations for enhancements (Wylie and Bauer 2002). During this analysis they identified positive and negative impacts to the community from tourism:

Positive Impacts	**Negative Impacts**
More money is entering the community	Dependence on tourism— no economic diversity
Relations with ANAM have improved	Training is limited to the same core group
Hunting and fishing in the national park have reduced	Community is dependent on a few people
Sanitary management has improved	Community is developing into a consumer society
Women have more value and are participating in the decision-making process	Individualism has been promoted by capitalism
Donations of equipment have been received	Culture is becoming a business
Social values have improved and alcoholism has reduced	Internal fights over roles of traditional government and tourism management

The Emberá have been providing sustainable tourism opportunities to locals and international tourists for just a few years. Their skill level is increasing as they receive more tourists and learn how best to meet their needs. They are asking for training and technical assistance to help them improve their skills and knowledge further. They are very aware of their culture and their local environment and how tourism might affect them in positive and negative ways. They feel that through sustainable tourism they can preserve their traditional way of life, protect the Chagres National Park, and improve their income and lifestyle. So far, it has been a great success.

Chapter 5

What Is Our Heritage?

Travel is fatal to prejudice, bigotry and narrow-mindedness.

Mark Twain, "Innocents Abroad," 1869

HERITAGE TOURISM: IN THE BEGINNING

Heritage tourism is often included under the banner "cultural and heritage tourism." The strong relationship between the concepts of "culture" and "heritage" makes it sometimes difficult to separate the two terms when referring to tourism experiences. In *Webster's II New College Dictionary* (2001 edition) "culture" is defined thus: "The totality of socially transmitted behavior patterns, arts, beliefs, institutions, and all other products of human work and thought typical of a population or community at a given time." In the same edition, "heritage" is defined thus: "(1) Property that is or can be inherited; (2) Something passed down from preceding generations; (3) The status gained by a person through birth." In this book, the terms are initially separated; however, I fully recognize that much of the literature on "cultural and heritage tourism," especially in terms of economic impact, lumps them together. I hope that the examples used in this chapter will help explain some of the differences, even though there can be advantages to merging the terms as far as tourism is concerned.[1]

Heritage tourism has been with us for a long time. It is hard truly to understand heritage tourism in the present and what it might develop into in the future without briefly looking at the past. Almost any vision we have for heritage tourism in the future is, in one way or another, a montage of images from yesterday.

Heritage tourism certainly dates back to classical antiquity—to ancient Greece and Rome and before. As early as 1600 BC, archaeologists tell us, visitors to the pyramids were scratching graffiti on them. On the underground tombs of the pharaohs in the Valley of the Kings were found the phrase "Palladius of Hermopolis—saw and was amazed."

Perhaps we should modify these words to "generations after us will visit the tombs of the pharaohs and be amazed, provided we have the good sense to preserve this precious legacy for those who come after us." Consider this: the seven wonders of the ancient world (the Great Pyramid of Giza, the Hanging Gardens of Babylon, the thirty-foot statue of Zeus at Olympia, the Temple of Artemis at Ephesus, the Mausoleum at Halicarnassus, the Colossus of Rhodes, and the Pharos at Alexandria)—the first well-known heritage tourist attractions, if you will—were all built by people.

Heritage tourism on a global scale has largely looked to the United Nations Educational, Scientific and Cultural Organization (UNESCO) for leadership. UNESCO's World Heritage program encourages travel to important cultural and historic destinations. Destinations the world over vie to get chosen for the World Heritage List. In 1978, the first twelve sites were inscribed on the World Heritage List; by 1987, there were already 289 sites on the list, and ten years later, in 1997, the list had almost doubled to 552 sites. Every year the World Heritage Committee includes more sites on the list based on their outstanding value. As a result global travelers can admire the wonders of the world, learn more about other countries, their environments, cultures, values, and ways of life, and hence increase their international understanding. A major challenge for world heritage conservation in the future is to encourage people to visit sites without inflicting damage. For example, the Great Wall of China was added to the World Heritage List in 1987. The brick- and stone-built sections of the Great Wall near Beijing, dating from the Ming dynasty, are visited by millions of local and foreign tourists every year. After all these years and the impact of tourist visits, some fragile parts of the Great Wall are in danger of collapse.

In the early 1990s, only a small number of U.S. states had state-wide heritage tourism programs. By 2002, more than half had cultural or heritage tourism programs, and the list continues to grow. Some states, such as North Carolina, are utilizing heritage tourism as a special stimulus for travelers who want to experience the authentic natural, historic, and cultural resources of a community or region. For example, North Carolina's Mountains-to-Sea Trail, which is currently under construction (a 1,000-mile corridor from one end of the state to the other), represents nature and heritage tourism. The state highlights its rich history and unique cultural attractions along this trail. As heritage tourism has evolved into the fastest-growing segment of the travel market it has become a major component of the economic development efforts of rural and metropolitan areas alike in North Carolina.

A second example featuring good marketing practices for heritage tourism is the Blue Ridge Heritage Initiative, a tripartite collaboration among North Carolina, Virginia, and Tennessee. The North Carolina Arts Council was awarded a challenge grant from the National Endowment for the Arts for economic development and cultural preservation in the counties that border the Blue Ridge Parkway. North Carolina enlisted assistance from the arts agencies of Virginia and Tennessee and other sponsors to produce the first two guidebooks highlighting heritage tourism destinations: *Blue Ridge Music Trails: Finding a Place in the Circle* by Fred C. Fussell (2003) and *Cherokee Heritage Trails Guidebook* by Barbara R. Duncan and Brett H. Riggs (2003).

The goal of the North Carolina Heritage Tourism Program is to cooperate with strategic partners to develop and support sustainable efforts that strive to protect, preserve, and promote the state's natural, historic, and cultural resources, thereby enhancing the economic well-being and quality of life of the local community. During the "2003 North Carolina Governor's Conference on Tourism," the North Carolina Division of Tourism, Film and Sports Development included a major agenda item entitled "Building Sustainable Partnerships for Nature and Culture Tourism."

HERITAGE TOURISM: TODAY AND TOMORROW

Recognizing and defining heritage tourism is an important aspect of the overall educational process. Case studies of successful community cooperation, especially some high-profile community projects, reinforce the need for many different partnerships in heritage tourism. Suggesting principles and concepts of heritage tourism adds immeasurably to the communication process so important to a project's overall success.

A growing aspect of heritage tourism is the competition among potential sites for the designation "National Heritage Area." In National Heritage Areas residents, businesses, and local government have joined together to conserve and celebrate the region's heritage. The U.S. Congress established twenty-seven National Heritage Areas around the country, and these encourage the protection of a wide variety of historic, environmental, scenic, and cultural resources in partnership with sustainable development for tourism and other economic opportunities (www.cr.nps.gov/heritageareas/). They educate residents and visitors about community history, traditions, and the environment, and provide for outdoor recreation. They are managed by partnerships among federal, state, and local governments and the private sector. A "management entity" is named by the U.S. Congress to coordinate the voluntary actions of the partners. A National Heritage Area allows historic and cultural sites in a region to partner with other historic sites, parks, businesses, governments, and communities the better to tell the unique story of a region. This draws attention to the relationships between sites and allows visitors to explore multiple sites during a stay. The U.S. Congress has defined a National Heritage Area as an area or corridor "where natural, cultural, historic, and recreational resources combine to form a cohesive, nationally distinctive landscape arising from patterns of human activity shaped by geography. These patterns make National Heritage Areas representative of the national experience through the physical features that remain and the traditions that have evolved in them."

At the time of writing in 2005, Kansas is seeking National Heritage Area recognition for twenty-seven counties in eastern Kansas that have joined together on the basis of a shared heritage. Current documentation seeks federal designation for an area it calls "Bleeding Kansas National Heritage Area in 2005" (Visitors and Convention Bureau, Lawrence, Kansas). For eastern Kansas the unique heritage known as Bleeding Kansas covers the important time period between 1854 and 1861, when Kansas became a state. Events in eastern Kansas at that time made the national news, prompted major congressional debates, and precipitated the American Civil War. Most interest in Civil War history focuses on events in the eastern United States. The important pre–Civil War story that took place on the Kansas prairie during this period has not received the recognition it deserves. Although the project concentrates on the Bleeding Kansas heritage, the twenty-seven counties also have a rich heritage in other connected and separate events. The fact that these counties have joined together to develop and promote heritage is in itself significant and is another example of "coopetition," as defined in Chapter 3. The plan is for these eastern Kansas counties, mostly in rural areas, to develop guided and self-guided tours throughout the region, add new interpretations and events, and safeguard significant buildings and land as part of preserving the area's sense of place. The initial goal was to have this National Heritage Area recognition take place in 2005, which would have also supported events and projects planned and underway to celebrate the 150th anniversary of the state of Kansas in 2011.

DEFINITIONS ARE GOOD

Heritage tourism appears to be gaining widespread acceptance as a part of the overall sustainable tourism effort and separately as a special attraction. Some communities are seeking to restore old buildings in an effort to preserve their historic legacy and to draw visitors to participate in the local heritage. Williamsburg, Virginia, is one example of an entire community being a replica of its history and heritage. Then, in Newport, Rhode Island, you can enjoy one of the finest collections of historic mansions in the United States. Newport's main heritage tourism product, the images of extravagant houses and the lifestyles of the rich and famous as depicted in *The Great Gatsby,* attracts over 1 million visitors annually.

Heritage tourism, more than any other component of sustainable tourism, crosses the boundaries between the natural environment, cultural tourism, and rural tourism. It is not easily definable, and as many definitions for heritage tourism can be found as there are experts in the field. Most U.S. researchers agree that the National Trust for Historic Preservation's Heritage Tourism Program (hereafter referred to as the Heritage Tourism Program) is a good beginning point for recognizing most of the attributes of heritage tourism in the United States. The Heritage Tourism Program provides leadership, education, and advocacy to save America's diverse historic places and to revitalize communities.

The Heritage Tourism Program provides the following simple definition: "Heritage tourism is traveling to experience the places and activities that authentically represent the stories and people of the past" (National Trust for Historic Preservation 1999, p. 1). Much emphasis is placed on the word "authentically." Heritage tourism has also been defined to include visitors from outside of the host community inspired by curiosity about the past. That is, many tourists want to learn about the history of notable people and the community where they grew up, emphasizing their appreciation and understanding of history. Most studies classify heritage tourism products into such categories as historic sites, archeological sites, war and battle sites, city centers, downtowns, neighborhoods, historic buildings, heritage trails, routes, or waterways, heritage structures, heritage artifacts, and related kinds of products.

Most programs recognize that properly planned, designed, and marketed heritage tourism projects can increase the numbers of visitors and their expenditures, which in turn can be used to support and foster heritage sites. In brief, it is tourist spending that often ensures the future of heritage tourism. It is this partnership between the "hosts" (providing quality heritage tourism) and the "guests" (enjoying heritage tourism) that is important to the quality of life of the community.

Behind all of the Heritage Tourism Program's activities are five guiding principles developed by the National Trust through a three-year initiative funded in part by the National Endowment for the Arts:

1. Collaborate
2. Find the fit between a community and tourism
3. Make sites and programs come alive
4. Focus on quality and authenticity
5. Preserve and protect resources (National Trust for Historic Preservation 2001, p. 3)

MODELING HERITAGE TOURISM

One of the most interesting reports on heritage tourism in the United States is "Experience and Benefits: A Heritage Tourism Development Model," based on a study conducted by the U.S. Department of Agriculture's Forest Service (1997). The report maintains that public land managers can benefit from a comprehensive, systematic approach toward heritage tourism based on learning from others in the industry. Specifically, the report was designed to help public land managers focus their heritage resource efforts on expanding the recreational and tourism opportunities provided to visitors. It was also intended to help managers develop quality heritage attractions that protect resources while providing valuable information and benefits to visitors. In an arrangement with the Heritage Tourism Program, the Forest Service initiated an analysis of the heritage tourism resources in the Four Corners area of the United States (Arizona, Colorado, New Mexico, and Utah).

> In an arrangement with the National Trust for Historic Preservation's Heritage Tourism Program, the Forest Service initiated an analysis of the heritage tourism resources in the Four Corners area of the United States. In this region, 2,292 heritage tourism sites were identified with 818 organizations responding. In this survey, 1,223 heritage providers were identified with 390 organizations responding. (USDA Forest Service 1997, p. 5)

The model developed from this project further indicates the need to manage the heritage aspects of sustainable tourism. The key management principle is to "balance visitor access to heritage sites with the maintenance of the integrity of the resource" (p. 15)—in essence, preserve the structures, include good interpretation of the site, and make sure it is there for future generations to enjoy. The report also issues an indirect message that tourists have responsibilities for protecting and preserving a site.

Heritage tourism programs are introducing many new concepts, such as getting the tourist to understand the heritage site better, educating the tourist on the need for protection and preservation, and obtaining support from the tourist to enhance the heritage site. For example, in southern Colorado, visitors can work side by side with archaeologists to preserve Anasazi ruins. Many universities have programs that help students become better aware of the importance of supporting local, state, and national heritage programs. East Carolina University, in Greenville, North Carolina, has a maritime studies program that involves students in investigating the historical and heritage aspects of shipwrecks from the North Carolina coast and beyond, including shipwrecks in rivers and along the coast of the U.S. Virgin Islands.

Often overlooked is the role that art history plays in heritage tourism. Kay Smith, Artist Laureate in the prestigious Lincoln Academy of Illinois and a widely recognized painter of historic sites, is indirectly impacting the promotion of heritage tourism through her interpretive art history programs. Her lectures about the history and heritage behind each of her paintings bring America to life through the eyes of an artist and through the words of a master storyteller, educator, and historian. Kay Smith has traveled the length and breadth of the United States to paint the nation's historic events and landmarks. Such efforts raise our consciousness about preserving our history before progress destroys all traces of our past; they also enable a better understanding of heritage tourism.

As the first case study in this book mentions, efforts are underway in St. Croix, U.S. Virgin Islands, to get the Salt River Bay National Historical Park and Ecological Preserve onto the World Heritage List. In addition, St. Croix is trying to have its historic landmarks from the earliest times of the native population to the Spanish, French, and Danish ownership of the island recognized as special heritage sites and destinations for heritage travelers. The economic history of the sugar plantations and the resulting slave trade are an integral part of the island's development. As a result of its history, St. Croix is developing a complete program that highlights its heritage tourism product.

A very interesting destination that has developed and marketed heritage tourism effectively is Jamaica. The island's "greathouses" are a prime example of its accomplishments in this area. Joann Biondi (1996), writing in the magazine *Caribbean Travel and Life,* says, "Jamaica's stately greathouses recall the days when sugar was king" (p. 83). Not unlike the conversion of "castles" into guesthouses in areas of Europe, Jamaica has restored many of its greathouses as places where travelers can overnight. "The period of greathouses in Jamaica took place between 1665 and 1838," according to Nadine Atkinson, a historian with the Jamaica National Heritage Trust (Biondi 1996, p. 84). Although these greathouses recall a time of tragic slavery in much of Jamaica, they also reflect the European influence on the area and add to an understanding of Jamaica's history. Many have been carefully restored to maintain their authenticity and integrity, providing an important history lesson for heritage travelers. One of the most interesting and popular of the greathouses is Rose Hall, the former home of Annie Palmer, who was nicknamed the White Witch of Rose Hall. She is alleged to have murdered many people in her Rose Hall residence over 170 years ago and to have returned to haunt the house. Jamaica has done an excellent job of restoring these homes as guesthouses and touring sites and seeks to market them as an integral part of its sustainable tourism program.

We can find many examples and success stories to illustrate good heritage tourism programs. One common thread of this success is usually the degree of community involvement in the project, as shown by the following case study.

CASE STUDY: LOOKING FOR LINCOLN— VANDALIA, ILLINOIS, DEVELOPS NEW LINCOLN PARK

A June 2001 tourism project developed in Vandalia, Fayette County, Illinois, illustrates many of the steps a community must take in developing heritage tourism. This rural community of some 7,000 people, located in central-southern Illinois, is on the right track to welcome heritage visitors. Although Vandalia is mainly a farming community, it has developed some light industry as well as embarking on a few tourism initiatives.

Vandalia's main claim to fame is as Illinois' capital (before the capital was transferred to Springfield in 1839), where state legislator Abraham Lincoln honed his political skills before becoming the sixteenth president of the United States. Lincoln, who as president would be faced with decisions that could bring the country together or tear it apart, spent some of his critical formative years in Vandalia, learning important values and political lessons. The Old State Capitol building, which houses the 1836 Vandalia Statehouse Historic Site, is the oldest existing state capitol building. Lincoln gave several speeches there, including his first protest against slavery in 1837. He also received his license to practice law within its walls. The impressive Federal-style building, with its high ceilings, tall windows, and vintage furnishings, has been carefully restored and is immaculately maintained. This Lincoln connection, which has the potential to attract an increased number of international visitors, is why Vandalia believed it important to honor Lincoln and in June 2001 unveiled a life-sized statue of Abraham Lincoln and dedicated a new Lincoln Park as part of the heritage of the community.

Some of what happened with respect to Vandalia's tourism program had its beginnings in 2000, when Vandalia became a part of the Illinois Main Street Program of the National Trust for Historic Preservation (referred to here simply as the Main Street program). This program, national in scope but local and state-level in application, encourages communities to improve their appearance within the context of historic preservation, add to their amenities, and improve the quality of life for local citizens. Vandalia City Council and other groups have taken a leadership role in helping to develop and promote heritage tourism throughout the area.

The Vandalia Main Street Design Committee listed some of the good things about Vandalia and its downtown business district, including the presence of the state capitol building; Vandalia's distinction as a terminus of the National Road (first interstate highway), which is highlighted by the Madonna of the Trail statue (one of thirteen in the country honoring the pioneer women who once traveled the National Road); a century-old church that houses the Fayette County Museum (chock-full of Lincoln-era memorabilia and items actually used by Lincoln); the Old State Cemetery, established by the State of Illinois in 1823; the Little Brick House (with historic furnishings); the impressive black granite piece that is the Farmers Monument; the presence of two major highways (Interstate 70 and U.S. Route 51); the city's location along the Kaskaskia River; and some local heritage festivals and events.

Lincoln Park did not just happen. It took a lot of hard work and commitment from community leaders and local citizens. The cost of the statue alone was $52,000. The Vandalia Main Street program was given the task of raising half this cost, with the other half coming from two state grants. Sixteen local citizens stepped forward with $1,000 apiece and other individuals, clubs, and businesses raised an additional $31,000. This generous outpouring allowed extra money for the park's development and a plaque recognizing the sixteen $1,000 contributors. The warden of the Vandalia Correctional Center arranged for work-camp inmates to help maintain Lincoln Park. Vandalia City Council, the Vandalia Tourism Commission, and many others gave their support. In addition, the Vandalia Main Street program engaged an Illinois Historic Preservation Agency architect to help with planning and streetscape design to improve Vandalia's downtown.

Abraham Lincoln is a popular national and international figure in the history of the United States, and Vandalia played an important role in his growth to prominence. It was in Vandalia that he learned his leadership skills and political savvy. Vandalia has an opportunity through the state tourism office to get the word out about its important Lincoln connection.

Vandalia already participates in cooperative tourism ventures such as the Looking for Lincoln program, which highlights the numerous Illinois connections to President Lincoln. It is a member of the eight-county Southwestern Illinois Tourism and Convention Bureau, which promotes tourism to the area, and Vandalia gets promoted domestically and internationally through the State of Illinois Tourism Office. The National Road, which was originally the old National Pike (running between Cumberland, Maryland, and Vandalia, Illinois), was recently designated an "All American Road." This recognition will help increase tourism in all the communities along the old National Pike.

These kinds of partnerships can help only if Vandalia continues to take strong initiatives and presents a quality tourism product. Taking advantage of every opportunity for exposure to potential tour operators, travel agents, and others in the tourism industry is vital. Vandalia is definitely on the path to obtaining the benefits of tourism in a sustainable way and further improving its heritage tourism products. With local, regional, and state cooperation, total commitment, and continued perseverance, Vandalia will be welcoming increasing numbers of visitors. Whether Vandalia will be successful in its tourism endeavors depends largely on good local leadership and strong community involvement.

Chapter 6

Culturally, Tourism Is Important

To us Sundance is and always will be a dream. What you see, smell, taste and feel here is a dream being carefully nurtured. It is an area whose pledge is to people. What we offer in the form of art and culture, spirit and service, is homegrown and available to all.

Robert Redford

WHAT IS CULTURAL TOURISM?

No truly universally accepted definition of cultural tourism exists. As mentioned in Chapter 5, *Webster's II New College Dictionary* defines "culture" thus: "The totality of socially transmitted behavior patterns, arts, beliefs, institutions, and all other products of human work and thought characteristic of a population or community at a given time." The "State of Missouri Cultural Tourism Development Plan" includes a "Cultural Tourism Definition" (Moskin and Guettler 1998, p. 1):

Cultural tourism is travel that is motivated entirely, or in part, by artistic, heritage or historical offerings. America's cultural resources offer domestic and international travelers the opportunity to experience what is uniquely American: our regional differences and ethnic character, our history and our most contemporary expression. It is a mosaic of places, traditions, celebrations, and experiences that portrays America and its people and reflects the diversity and character of the United States.

Many other definitions of cultural tourism can be found that depend to a large extent on the locale and on the perspective of the entity providing them. From a narrow tourism point of view, cultural tourism is most often associated with the arts, humanities, museums, festivals, food, music, theater, and special celebrations. But the concept of cultural tourism overlaps, certainly at the local level, with heritage tourism.

The activities for the National Lewis and Clark Bicentennial Commemoration in 2004-2006 provide a good example of the frequent blending of cultural, heritage, and rural tourism. An estimated 25 million travelers will camp, drive, bike, paddle, ride, or walk in the explorers' footsteps to partake in national heritage and culture events, mostly in rural areas. Certainly this Lewis and Clark odyssey is important as a nature, heritage, and culture travel experience. The diversity and richness of the many Native American tribal experiences associated with the journey and the journals of the participants of the Lewis and Clark expedition suggest a legacy of exploration and culture-related travel. Although the U.S. National Park Service, the lead agency for the commemoration activities, has done a good job in supporting some of the developmental programs, it has failed to help the local communities understand the marketing of their cultural/heritage tourism products or how to provide the services required for a quality tourism experience. As a result, many communities are not prepared for the tourists who will visit their area.

The best discussion of the similarities and differences of cultural and heritage tourism I have come across is contained in the National Trust for Historic Preservation's (2001b) article "Cultural and Heritage Tourism—The Same, or Different?"

> It is not possible to define cultural tourism and heritage tourism as two entirely different kinds of tourism. In looking at definitions of both heritage and cultural tourism, there clearly is overlap between the two. Without question, the areas of overlap far exceed the differences. . . . An informal survey of programs across the country reveals that "heritage" programs are more often found in rural areas while "cultural" programs are more often found in urban settings. Historic preservation groups are more likely to describe "heritage tourism" programs, while museum and arts groups are more likely to refer to "cultural tourism" programs, though the content is often quite similar. . . . The primary difference between the two is that heritage tourism is

"place" based. Heritage tourism programs create a sense of place rooted in the local landscape, architecture, people, artifacts, traditions and stories that make a particular place unique. Cultural tourism programs celebrate the same kinds of experiences, though with less emphasis on place. Thus, viewing the work of a great master artist in his home and studio is a heritage tourism experience, while viewing those same pieces of art in a traveling exhibition is a cultural tourism experience. The content is the same while the context is different. . . . This distinction clarifies why preservationists refer to "heritage tourism" while museums and arts organizations are more likely to use the term "cultural tourism." Historic preservation tends to address the built environment and cultural landscape, and preservationists place a high value on maintaining the original context. On the other hand, museums and the arts are more likely to work with collections and performances that can be transported and shared with other communities. . . . While using the term "cultural heritage tourism" is useful to help bring together all of the partners that need to be working together on this type of an effort (including organizations and individuals representing the arts, museums, the humanities, historic preservation, heritage areas, ethnic groups and others including tourism partners), it is cumbersome to use in marketing programs to potential visitors. An informal survey reveals that the terms "cultural" and "heritage" have different meaning for the layperson—and for your potential visitors. Thus, based on your audience, it may be more effective to use one term or the other depending upon the image that you are trying to convey.[1]

I have written separate chapters for heritage tourism and cultural tourism, but I recognize the overlap and confusion, and the impossibility of always clearly delineating the two terms. Of particular concern is trying to differentiate "heritage tourism" and "cultural tourism" in the tourism statistics. For example, a 2003 Travel Industry Association of America report, *The Historic/Cultural Traveler,* indicated that 118 million Americans are considered historic or cultural travelers.

WHAT ARE OUR PROBLEMS WITH CULTURE?

It is clear that tourism has led, in a short time, to a closer association and mingling of people of different races, creeds, religions, and cultures. However, concern is growing that mass international tourism may have a detrimental impact on local cultures and customs or that an area will distort its festivals and ceremonies to stage spectacles for the benefit of visitors. Thus, some people believe that tourism leads to the disappearance of traditional human environments and replaces them with towers of artificial concrete, ideas, ethics, and morals—in effect, threatening the whole fabric of tradition and nature. As such distortions arise, the concern is that the worlds of host and guest will separate, leading to greater prejudices and misunderstandings. In the classic travel book *The Golden Hordes,* John Ash and Louis Turner (1976) contend that tourism is a form of cultural imperialism, an unending pursuit of fun, sun, and sex by the golden hordes of pleasure seekers who are damaging local cultures and polluting the world in their quest. (Aspects of this concern are as valid today as they were in the 1970s, when the book was written.) Ash and Turner felt that too much "tourism" would damage the local culture of the host country, pervert traditional social values, encourage prostitution and hustling among "the natives," and usually result in a proliferation of fabricated tourist-oriented cultural performances and the sale of cheap souvenirs masquerading as local arts and crafts.

Other articles mention that the local population may be hostile toward tourists because of the outlandish requirements for accommodations and services or the unreasonable demands of a limited number of rude and arrogant visitors (Zeigler 1991). This may account for some countries' lack of interest in providing tourists with an authentic cultural tourism product. Another issue is that tourist facilities in many developing countries are under foreign ownership and management, which may create the feeling that indigenous people perform only menial tasks and have no cultural base. Not infrequently, resort development has resulted in local people being denied access to their own beaches. Tourism may also be regarded as a threat to the indigenous cultures and mores, or to the standard of local arts and crafts as efforts are made to expand output to meet tourists' demands. All these factors can seriously skew the perception of tourists and can sometimes lead to demands for the flow of visitors to be curbed. For these reasons and others cited in this chapter and throughout this book, it is important to have a sustainable tourism management plan.

Finally, too often we read articles about the continuing desecration of cultural sites. A story in *The New York Times* for May 23, 2003, reported that the Iraq war had created a situation where looters were "tearing into Iraqi archaeological sites, stealing urns, statues, vases and cuneiform tablets that often date back 3,000 years and more to Babylon and Sumer, archaeologists say" (Andrews 2003, p. A1). Too rapid industrial progress, wars, natural disasters, commercial opportunism, and uninformed populations have had detrimental impacts on cultural treasures and, hence, cultural tourism over the centuries. This situation needs to be rectified through improved international management systems and educational programs before priceless pieces of the world's culture disappear forever, thereby impacting cultural travel. Certainly, actions by the World Heritage Organization are a step in the right direction, but it is an underfunded institution with little international authority.

AVOIDING THE PITFALLS

The numerous incidents where tourism does impact negatively on an area are not inevitable. Alongside its economic benefits, a carefully planned, well-organized tourist destination can benefit area residents by exposing them to a variety of ideas, people, languages, and other cultural traits. It can add to the richness of a resident's experience by stimulating an interest in the area's history through restoration and preservation of historic sites.

For example, the revival of some U.S. African-American communities as potential tourism resources or destinations is based on their cultural richness. In New York, the revitalization of Harlem has made it a destination for foreign tourists, and the myths, realities, folklore, and legacies of Harlem are now known around the world. Harlem is coming to be recognized, both domestically and internationally, for its rich cultural heritage, landmarks, museums, churches, parks, architectural structures, and varied nightlife.

Organized cultural tourism development can provide opportunities for local people to learn more about themselves. This may increase feelings of pride in their heritage and result in a heightened perception of their own worth. For example, residents of Mexico City speak with great pride about their Ballet Folklorico, their National Museum of Anthropology, and their Palace of Fine Arts. The Venezuelans speak affectionately about "La Feria de San Sebastian," a great festive event with cultural and other exciting celebrations that result in Venezuelan participation and foreign interest and visitation.

Even a highly localized cultural event such as "Buffalo Bill Cody Days," a commemorative occasion when the residents of Leavenworth, Kansas, celebrate their historical link to William F. (Buffalo Bill) Cody (1846-1917), can be a positive cultural experience for nonresidents as well. The local "Potomac Days Parade" in Potomac, Maryland, has grown into an international festival where people from many different backgrounds from Korea to Lithuania show off traditional clothes, food, and arts and crafts. Kansas City has a similar annual international event, the Ethnic Enrichment Festival, which grows bigger each year. Other local festivals often relate to important local traditions, such as the annual "corn festival" in Vandalia, Illinois. The local community in Greenville, North Carolina, has partnered with East Carolina University to celebrate the rich culture of several nationalities in an International Festival in April. Dubois, Wyoming, involves the entire community in its full day of activities during a very special celebration of the Fourth of July; a major highway is blocked off for a unique parade that passes by such interesting sites as the Rustic Pine Tavern and Cowboy Café. These local celebrations started gradually but have grown into regular annual celebrations that both residents and visitors look forward to.

According to the Travel Industry Association of America's Travel Poll (n.d.), 41 percent of U.S. adults attended a festival while on a trip away from home in 2002. This translates to more than 59.5 million U.S. adults. Such festivals add greatly to local communities' economic, cultural, and social goals. Globally, the number one country for international visitors is France, which has, for several decades, stressed its cultural values to tourists (Spain is second and the United States is third) (World Tourism Organization, 2005). In 2004, Paris, which promotes to the world its many cultural and heritage attractions, was one of the leading international culture sites.

Tourism can also contribute to cultural revival. Often, the demand by tourists for local arts and crafts has heightened the interest and preserved the skills of local artisans and craftspeople by providing an audience and market for their art. In the United States, a number of Native American ceremonies and dances owe their continued existence to the fact that tourists were interested in them, which stimulated many local Native Americans to revive them and teach their meaning to the new generations. This preservation of culture, whether in local artifacts or religious rites, forms the history of an area or country. The very uniqueness of a culture is frequently the primary tourism attraction. It contributes to the quality of life of both the residents and tourists, but it is often the tourists who provide the interest and economic means to preserve a cultural activity.

One important way to avoid cultural tourism problems is better education, not only in the form of travel information or site guides, but also through such programs as Flinders University's (Australia) Bachelor of Cultural Tourism. The reason one should study cultural tourism at Flinders University is contained in the program description:

> Tourism has become a more sophisticated business and modern tourists more discerning. A high proportion travel not just to see new places, but to learn about their cultures and the people's way of life. They do not want to feel part of a mass market and have high expectations about the level of service and information they will receive. It is vital, therefore, that our tourism industry is run by professionals who understand the mechanics of the industry and the phenomenon of tourism and also are able to interpret and highlight a destination's distinctive cultural features—from its heritage to its lifestyle.

WHAT ARE THE PRIORITIES OF ACTION?

Local and state arts, humanities, and museum agencies play a major role in the development, preservation, and promotion of cultural tourism activities by providing study tours, informational displays and guides, video or audiotapes, educational classes and lectures, and other measures to increase the quality of the visit for tourists. Such efforts benefit the community and local residents, too. In the United States, for example, we have the important national *Partners in Tourism: Culture and Commerce* report, which provides information on "six regional cultural tourism leadership forums" (Garfield 1997). These forums included representatives from the thousands of museums, performing arts festivals, and cultural events that take place each year across this nation. Such cultural tourism activities engender both enjoyment and learning through authentic encounters with the arts, with history, and with cultural traditions both past and present.

Through these six forums, *Partners in Tourism* identified four major priorities:

1. Creating sustainable and fruitful partnerships among the various stakeholders of cultural tourism
2. Preserving cultural integrity, remaining true to the authentic story being told, and being faithful to the cultural organization's mission
3. Involving the community in the cultural tourism development process
4. Acquiring credible and consistent research demonstrating the social and economic impact of cultural tourism

Major efforts are underway to better educate the public and researchers on sustainable tourism that includes specific reference to cultural tourism. For example, in 2002 National Geographic Traveler and the Travel Industry Association of America (2002) released *The Geotourism Study,* which expanded the concept of sustainability as it relates to cultural heritage tourism. Geotourism as defined by this study encompasses the preservation of a destination's culture, heritage, aesthetics, and environment, as well as the vitality of the community's lifestyles and economy. In addition, in 2003 the National Geographic Society launched a new "Sustainable Tourism Destinations Center," with a special subsection on "Culture and Heritage," for tourism professionals, travelers, and residents. The March 2004 issue of *National Geographic Traveler* contains a rating of selected sustainable tourism destinations across the globe with "culture" as one of the rating criteria.

A national organization that has been a long-time supporter of cultural tourism, largely as it relates to the arts, is the National Endowment for the Arts (NEA), headquartered in Washington, DC. The NEA was a supporter of the White House Conference on Travel and Tourism, which defines cultural tourism thus: "Travel directed toward experiencing the arts, heritage and special character of a place." Cultural tourism in this context includes visits to museums, arts festivals, heritage areas, performances, historic buildings, and authentic cultural attractions with the aim of educating and entertaining travelers. The NEA has also led the formation of partnerships between the cultural, commercial, and public sectors and communities, states, and regions to create cultural tourism enterprises. Such efforts will go a long way toward the overall management and promotion of quality cultural tourism experiences for tourists to enjoy for a long time into the future.

One of the largest cultural events in recent history took place from May 9 to September 26, 2004, in Barcelona, Spain. This five-month-long "Universal Forum of Cultures" featured 141 days of concerts, theater, symposia, dance, cabaret shows, open-air markets, marching bands, street performers, film festivals, and more. Much of the activity took place in and around Barcelona's new International Convention Center, which has a capacity of 15,000.

The following case study looks at the Cahokia Mounds State Historic Site near Collinsville, Illinois. The Cahokia Indians were an amazing group of people and one of the most interesting Native American cultures in the United States. They developed the city of Cahokia, which was inhabited from AD 700 to 1400.

CASE STUDY: EARLY NATIVE AMERICANS— CAHOKIA MOUNDS STATE HISTORIC SITE

Among the most fascinating archaeological treasures in the United States, and an important cultural tourism product, are the Cahokia Mounds. The remains of the most sophisticated prehistoric American Indian civilization north of Mexico are preserved at Cahokia Mounds State Historic Site. Within the 2,200-acre tract, located a few miles west of Collinsville, Illinois, lie the archaeological remains of the central section of the ancient city that is today known as Cahokia.

In 1982, the United Nations Educational, Scientific and Cultural Organization (UNESCO) designated Cahokia Mounds a World Heritage Site for its importance to our understanding of the prehistory of North America. Most of the following information is developed from information and brochures provided by the Illinois Historic Preservation Agency, which manages Cahokia Mounds, and from a series of newspaper articles in the *St. Louis Post-Dispatch* (January 9, 2000, pp. A1, A6-7).

According to archaeological finds, the city of Cahokia was inhabited from AD 700 to 1400. At its peak, from AD 1100 to 1200, the city covered nearly six square miles and had a population as large as 20,000 (roughly the number in London at that time) in extensive residential sections. Houses were arranged in rows and around open plazas, and the main agricultural fields lay outside the city.

The site is named for a subtribe of the Illini Indians, the Cahokia, who occupied the area when the French arrived in the late 1600s. What its ancient inhabitants called the city is unknown, since the site was abandoned well before European contact. Instead, archaeological investigations and scientific tests have provided what is known of the once-thriving Indian community.

The fate of the prehistoric Cahokians and their city is unknown. Depletion of resources probably contributed to the city's decline. A climate change after AD 1200 may have affected crop production and the plant and animal resources needed to sustain a large population. War, disease, social unrest, and declining political and economic power may have also taken their toll. A gradual decline in population began sometime after AD 1200, and by the 1400s the site had been abandoned.

Prehistoric Indians of the Late Woodland culture first inhabited Cahokia Mounds ca. AD 700. Living in compact villages, they hunted, fished, gathered wild plants for food, and cultivated gardens. This was not untypical of life for many Native American tribes during this time period.

Between AD 800 and 1000 another culture emerged, called Mississippian (Woodland and Mississippian are names assigned by archaeologists; they are not tribal names). Mississippians developed an agricultural system with corn, squash, and several seed-bearing plants (sunflower, marsh elder, lambs quarter, may grass, knotweed, little barley) as the principal crops. The stable food base enabled them to develop a very complex community with a highly specialized social, political, and religious organization. Cahokia became a regional center for the Mississippian culture after AD 900, with many outlying hamlets and villages. Major satellite towns were located near the modern communities of Mitchell, Dupo, Lebanon, East St. Louis, and St. Louis.

Originally there were more than 120 mounds, but the locations of only 109 have been recorded. Many were altered or destroyed by modern farming and urban construction. About sixty-eight are preserved within the historic site boundaries.

The mounds are made entirely of earth. The soil was transported on people's backs in baskets to the mound construction site. Most mounds show evidence of several construction stages. The diggings left large depressions called borrow pits, which still can be seen in the area. It is estimated that the Indians moved over 50 million cubic feet of earth for mound construction alone.

Cahokians constructed three types of mounds. The most common was the platform mound, whose flat top served as a base for ceremonial buildings or the residences of the elite. Two other types of mounds—conical and ridge-top—apparently were used for burials of important people or to mark important locations. However, the mounds were principally used for ceremonial activities; only a few were used for burials as most Cahokians were probably buried in cemeteries.

The great platform mound at Cahokia—Monks Mound, composed of an estimated 22 million cubic feet of earth—is the largest Indian mound north of Mexico and the largest known prehistoric earthen construction in the United States. It was built in several stages, mostly between AD 900 and 1200.

Monks Mound was named for the French Trappist monks who lived nearby in the early 1800s. Its base covers over fourteen acres, and it rises in four terraces to a height of one hundred feet. A massive building—105 feet long, 48 feet wide, and approximately 50 feet high—stood on the summit. There the principal ruler lived, conducted ceremonies, and governed the city.

Excavation of a small ridge-top mound—Mound 72—revealed nearly 300 ceremonial and sacrificial burials, mostly of young women, in mass graves. The Cahokians worshiped the sun and referred to their leader as a "sun god." The main burial appears to be that of a male ruler about forty-five years of age, laid on a blanket of more than 20,000 marine shell disc beads. Near him lay the remains of others sacrificed to serve him in the next life and a large cache of grave offerings. The skeletons of four men with their heads and hands missing were found near the largest sacrificial pit, which held the skeletons of fifty-three women between the ages of fifteen and twenty-five years. Several other mass burials were also uncovered.

The center of the city was surrounded by a two-mile long stockade—a wall of posts set in trenches, with projecting bastions (guard towers) every seventy feet. The stockade was constructed four times, and each construction took nearly 20,000 logs. Built for defense, it also served as a social barrier, segregating the more sacred precinct and the elite who lived there. Several sections of the stockade have been reconstructed.

Archaeological excavations have partially uncovered remains of four (possibly five) circular sun calendars that once consisted of large, evenly spaced log posts. These calendars, called woodhenges because of their functional similarity to Stonehenge in England, were probably used to determine the changing seasons and certain ceremonial periods important to an agricultural way of life. Constructed ca. AD 1000, they are an impressive example of Indian science and engineering.

Today, archaeologists fight to preserve the history of the Cahokians. Unfortunately, the Cahokia Mounds are in a highly developed area with dense commercial traffic. However, this important site may survive because of its unique history, increasing attention from tourists, and the efforts of preservationists and others interested in history. Its ultimate survival will depend on some of the good management techniques advocated in this book and on political support and community involvement.

Chapter 7

Tourism Goes Country

Healthy, free, the world before me . . . strong and content, I travel the open road.

Walt Whitman, "Song of the Open Road," 1856

TOURISM TO RURAL AREAS

Rural America was the first tourism development frontier and it is also the last (with many changes having taken place in between). The visionary President Thomas Jefferson initiated the first major governmental efforts for rural development with travel connotations. During his First Inaugural Address in 1801, he spoke of "[a] rising nation, spread over a wide and fruitful land . . . advancing rapidly to destinies beyond the reach of mortal eye." In 1803, he asked the U.S. Congress to approve an expedition from Wood River, Illinois, to the Pacific Ocean headed by Meriwether Lewis and William Clark. By the time their travels began, President Jefferson had authorized the Louisiana Purchase, which enlarged the tasks of the Lewis and Clark expedition to include establishing the "development" and "sustainability" of the lands they were to explore. Lewis and Clark learned from the Native Americans along their route that most tribes subscribed to one concept or another of sustainability of the lands, including flora, fauna, water, and spiritual values. After the expedition came the trappers, explorers, and travelers, many of whom had a great appreciation for the beauty of the West and a sincere concern for its protection. At the end of the 1800s, new conservation policies were enunciated by President Theodore Roosevelt that led to the development and protection of the parks and forests that now dot the modern American landscape and are an integral part of rural tourism. Rural travel destinations still offer the most diversity in terms of beauty, experience, culture, and heritage. Rural areas offer great opportunities for heritage tourism, ecotourism, and agritourism.

The success of tourism in the rural United States depends substantially on the recognition of a critical mass of local activities and attractions to enable tourism leaders to plan and manage a region's tourism economy effectively, to form partnerships, and to maximize the ability to capture tourist expenditures. Unfortunately, many rural communities have been hampered in these efforts by a lack of the human, financial, and technical resources necessary to establish a sustainable tourism industry acceptable to residents, businesspeople, and traveling guests alike. Many rural areas are looking toward instituting the idea that sustainable tourism resources can be effective tools of economic development and viability. Tourism is a highly workable option precisely because its success relies on an area's cultural, historic, ethnic, geographic, and natural uniqueness.

One state that has recognized these deficiencies and has chosen to meet the challenge head on is North Carolina. In cooperation with the North Carolina Arts Council, entities such as the North Carolina Cooperative Extension Service, the Golden LEAF Foundation, HomegrownHandmade, and the Duplin County Cooperative Extension are organizing rural areas into consumer-friendly trails, promoting agricultural tourism, and improving tourism structures and services. Trails will be self-directed driving routes throughout the state and will lead travelers to local areas of interest. A day's driving may include experiencing a farm operation (homegrown) or visiting a local pottery studio (handmade). In 2004, North Carolina State University and the Cooperative Extension Service hosted the Fourth Annual Agri-Cultural Tourism Conference to discuss opportunities in some rural areas. The new state office of Agritourism was introduced during this meeting, signaling new directions for rural tourism in North Carolina.

Rural areas also are realizing how effectively they can market their rural tourism products using e-commerce tools. The Center for Sustainable Tourism at the University of Colorado at Boulder highlights some of these Internet-based opportunities in its practical, no-nonsense "A Guide to New Technology for Rural Tourism Operators" (Center for Sustainable Tourism 2000). East Carolina University's new Institute for Tourism is helping some rural areas to develop "strategic tourism plans" or other mechanisms that emphasize their sustainable tourism products.

Although most Americans today live in metropolitan areas, the rural sectors of the United States have advanced in many ways over the years. Substantial improvements in and expansion of utilities, telecommunications, and the interstate highway system have placed rural America in a better position to serve both its population and visitors. Rural environments have vast expanses of land and water and wide diversity in their mountains, plains, forests, grasslands, and deserts that provide outstanding settings for leisure and recreational pursuits and are the primary commodities for a basic tourism product. In addition to stimulating rural economies, tourism can help preserve the environment in which it operates.

Rural areas also offer plentiful opportunities to visit large and well-maintained state and national parks. Many rural areas have lakes, rivers, and streams for boating, fishing, and swimming, and special habitats are being set aside for hiking and hunting.

The U.S. Forest Service has made great strides in linking forest preserves with the interests of the local population and out-of-town visitors. The Brooks Lake area near Dubois, Wyoming, on the way to Yellowstone National Park is a prime example. In addition to excellent trout fishing, the area has numerous well-developed campsite facilities, hiking trails, and other outdoor activities, providing a wide range of attractions for visitors, from fishing areas to historic sites to scenic mountains.

VALUABLE TOURISM PRODUCTS

Sometimes the question of just why rural areas should seek to attract tourists is raised. What really is the value of tourism to rural areas? To answer this question, we need to start with the overall value of tourism in the United States and then review opportunities for rural communities to participate in this growth opportunity.

According to the Travel Industry Association of America (TIA is the umbrella organization representing all facets of tourism in the United States), overall traveler spending by domestic and international visitors in the United States in 2004 was more than $600 billion, up from $555 billion in 2003. Projections for 2005 indicate an additional 5.6 percent increase that would bring expenditures to $634 billion. The forecast also reported that two of the hardest-hit segments in the travel industry, domestic business travel and international inbound travel, will both see their first increases since before the September 11, 2001, tragedy, as 2004 business trips reached nearly 144 million and are likely to increase another 3.6 percent to 149 million in 2005. International arrivals to the United States rose above 7.5 percent in 2004 and are forecast to increase 5 percent in 2005. Following several years of decline, international travel to the United States appears to be vibrant and showing healthy growth. The world economy (including the United States) appears to be rebounding somewhat in 2005 as improved safety and security measures are in place and people are "in the skies" and "on the road again."

Small towns across America are beginning to realize that the development potential offered by tourism is attainable if they market their communities. Domestic and international visitors have expressed an interest in seeing rural America, often on tourism routes or theme itineraries linking historical, cultural, and natural attractions. This interest has an economic multiplier effect in a variety of travel industry sectors—for example, support for heritage areas and bus companies bringing travelers to rural sections of the United States (particularly to areas such as Branson, Missouri), the enhancement of Scenic Byways travel programming, and the conscientious integration of recreation and its by-products, such as recreational vehicular travel, with sustainable tourism development in rural areas. The income generated by rural tourism, however modest, can be utilized to revitalize the community and encourage further economic investment. Tourism is a viable economic development alternative for rural communities, not least in creating jobs and incomes for rural residents, but it must be designed and developed in a sustainable way in order to ensure a continuing high-quality experience for the visitor.

In 2001, the U.S. Department of Agriculture commissioned an important study at Brigham Young University on international visitors to rural areas in the United States. One result of this effort is a book, *Best Practices Guidebook for International Tourism Development for Rural Communities* (Edgell 2002), that addresses important rural tourism issues and concerns. The book concludes that rural areas interested in the potential benefits from tourism need to plan and implement carefully programs that appeal to the special interests of visitors.[1]

Some states have recognized the need to be innovative and creative in the development of rural tourism. Agritourism is an area of special opportunity, and North Carolina, for example, which has seen increased interest in rural tourism, is taking advantage of its agricultural heritage to develop and promote agritourism. Kansas likewise has recognized the importance of rural tourism and is emphasizing agritourism. Much agritourism is farm based. In some cases tourists actually perform farm chores as part of the program. In other cases, they simply take advantage of the recreation opportunities that some farms offer, or they may stay at a rural bed-and-breakfast facility that provides special recreation in a rural setting.

David Fogarty and Mitch Renkow, in an article titled "Agritourism Opportunities for North Carolina," have looked at the various aspects and value of developing agritourism. They point out that in North Carolina

> agritourism already exists in a wide range of on-farm recreation and hospitality businesses. Examples of the activities offered by these businesses include farm tours, farm bed and breakfasts, wineries, petting zoos, fee hunting, fee fishing, farm vacations, horseback riding, and camping.

They also analyze the market for agritourism, its economic impact, its advantages and disadvantages, steps for developing agritourism, and a number of related issues.

Many universities, particularly in Europe, have rural tourism-related programs. Probably the best-known program in the United States is that of the Minnesota Extension Service and the Tourism Center at the University of Minnesota, which includes workshops, consultations, and community tourism assessments in rural areas. The Tourism Center offers excellent resources to help community leaders and educators understand agritourism and other aspects of rural tourism.

Several years ago the U.S. government, through the U.S. Department of Commerce, commissioned a "National Policy Study on Rural Tourism and Small Business Development." The report suggested a need for a strong governmental leadership role in rural tourism development. Acting on this research and other information, the U.S.

Congress enacted the Export Promotion Act of 1992 (PL 102-372), which authorized and created the National Rural Tourism Foundation as a charitable and nonprofit corporation charged with "the planning, development, and implementation of projects and programs which have the potential to increase travel and tourism export revenues by attracting foreign visitors to rural America" (PL 102-372, p. 3). However, the lack of "seed money" funding by the government means that the foundation has been unable to provide services. To date, the U.S. government has not really stepped forward to provide comprehensive rural tourism policy and guidelines or to fund rural tourism development. As mentioned in Chapter 6, a wonderful opportunity to offer special technical assistance and guidelines for rural tourism marketing and promotion was missed by the U.S. Department of the Interior in its planning and implementation of the Lewis and Clark commemoration activities for 2004-2006. However, Congress is considering legislation that could assist a broad range of rural programs, including rural tourism development.

THE DYNAMICS OF THE TOURISM INDUSTRY

Today's hospitality and tourism agenda poses some dynamic challenges for those rural communities launching new tourism products. Customers are demanding higher-quality experiences, greater variety, and more flexibility in their travels. Many rural communities are responding to these demands, and they are finding better ways of marketing their products to a broad range of potential visitors by capitalizing on new technological advances in e-commerce and more effective database marketing (especially niche marketing).

The dynamics of the new marketplace sometimes challenge the development of sustainable tourism in rural areas. For the visitor, it is often the natural environment and the built environment, including historic buildings, local culture, and heritage and ecotourism sites, that are the initial attraction. Overdevelopment may conflict with environmental protection/preservation as rural communities prepare for tourism opportunities. However, the sustainable tourism approaches outlined in this book suggest important new directions and chart realistic courses of action that can be effectively implemented in both rural and urban areas.

One of the most energetic rural tourism development programs is the Scenic Byways program, aimed at getting people to travel on many of our rustic rural roads, scenic highways, and historic roadways. Other local programs, state programs, and national programs are dedicated to promoting the same notion. The Intermodal Surface Transportation Efficiency Act of 1991 included a "National Scenic Byways Program" to encourage the planning, design, and development of state scenic byways programs. Such efforts have gone a long way toward increasing rural tourism.

COMMUNITY INVOLVEMENT
MAKES FOR SUCCESSFUL TOURISM

Almost every rural area in the United States has some resource, attraction, activity, event, or special interest or adventure opportunity that can motivate a traveler. It may be a special fishing hole, a unique place for photography or painting, a backpacking or horseback trail, a good location for ballooning, a white-water rafting river, some unusual festival, a sporting event, a heritage tourism activity, or a cultural celebration. The point is that hardly any rural location is not conducive to some type of tourism. Even if the community is not the primary destination, it still may have tourism potential. It may be on a favorite route for travelers and thus provide gasoline, food, lodging, souvenirs, and other services and products to visitors. Alternatively, the area may not yet be an important travel destination, but may have the potential to develop tourism products and services that support a tourism destination. Whatever the case, no tourism product should be developed or marketed without the involvement and support of the local residents. If they are not included in the beginning, do not expect them to help at a later date.

Market studies suggest that international visitors want to see the "real America," referring to rural areas and people. The potential of tourism has prompted many communities to develop an economy around the activities and needs of the traveling public. The level of development varies with each community's needs and expectations.

Developing an economy around tourism can bring many benefits to a community. However, that development will have the costs and liabilities associated with almost any industry within a small community. Residents must determine whether the benefits from these new industries, including tourism, will be worth the costs involved. Whether a community should try to develop tourism and what type of development would be best suited to the community can be determined only after a careful study of community interest, specific community needs that tourism could meet, and the costs and benefits of tourism to the community.

A good inventory of potential tourism resources is critical to the success of any rural tourism project. Most communities have a variety of attractions that do or could draw visitors to their area and most, if not all, communities could increase the number of tourists to their area.

- *Historic attractions* include battlefields, cemeteries, old forts, birthplaces of famous people, pioneer homes, and locations of special events. Such attractions will draw large numbers of tourists if the features are significant and if they are packaged and promoted.
- *Natural, scenic, or environmental features* include the mountains, rivers, lakes, forests, farms, springs, beaches, and wildlife in the area. These attractions and the activities associated with them, such as hiking, sightseeing, photography, hunting, fishing, and nature study, can attract large numbers of visitors if the opportunities are packaged and the features are of high quality.
- *Cultural and ethnic attractions* include unique lifestyles, archaeological sites, art galleries, early settlements, museums, and cultural center activities. They are popular with many tourists: interest in the cultural and ethnic features of people and communities attracts thousands of visitors to some places. Recent studies by the Travel Industry Association of America suggest this category is a high-growth area in today's marketplace.
- *Special events* include community-sponsored activities designed to entertain, educate, or allow tourists to participate. These events, which often reach a wide audience, may be connected to the history, culture, and natural features of the community or simply be a creation of the sponsoring group. Special events are

growing in popularity as tourist attractions and most communities have the potential to use special events and festivals to draw tourists to their areas.

A community may have some or all of these categories of attractions; however, in order to make decisions about their strength an inventory and assessment of the products should be conducted.

We can find many local community success stories in rural tourism development and promotion throughout the United States and globally as well. Branson, Missouri, for example, has developed into a year-round tourism destination drawing more than 7 million visitors annually. Other destinations may be more seasonal or directly connected to a special event or festival. For example, in 2001, Marceline, Missouri, held a centenary celebration of the birth of Walt Disney. Although Walt Disney was not born there, he spent an important part of his childhood in Marceline, giving the townspeople a good excuse for their birthday celebration. Almost 50,000 people (including international visitors) showed up in this town of 2,600 to share in the celebration—a true rural tourism festival success story.

Another increasingly popular agritourism event (or fad) in the new millennium is the "maize craze" that is sweeping America (and may have a basis in movies going as far back as *Field of Dreams* [1989]). Farmers set off several acres of their cornfields that are then custom cut into specially designed "mazes." Young people in particular enjoy searching for friends throughout the cornfield maze. In one small community in Wisconsin, over 50,000 people visited during the season, and the activity is also becoming popular in Iowa, Kansas, and many other states. The potential revenue can be substantial at $5 a person: with 10,000 people you generate $50,000. Some locations have local products that can be bought on site and out-of-town visitors spend money on other items throughout the local community.

If a rural area conducts an inventory of its potential tourism products, assesses their marketability, develops local leadership and tourism skills, educates the community about a chosen activity, and promotes an event, festival, or destination, it has a good chance of success. However, to "sustain" the area as a tourism destination it is important that the community conduct economic, environmental, and social impact studies throughout the process. The key is to maintain a sustainable tourism destination and to ensure that it adds to the quality of life of the local residents.

CASE STUDY: ROANOKE RIVER PADDLE TRAIL— A "WATERY" APPROACH TO RURAL TOURISM

One of the newest paddle trails in the United States is located in northeastern North Carolina on the Roanoke River. The brown-water river's headwaters are in the Blue Ridge Mountains of Virginia, and it eventually flows into the Atlantic Ocean by way of the historic towns of Weldon, Halifax, Hamilton, Windsor, Williamston, and Plymouth and the Albemarle Sound. The riverside village of Halifax, North Carolina, became the first colony to have citizens declare independence from England when residents signed the Halifax Resolves in April 1776. Later, the river saw fierce Civil War battles fought at Fort Branch and Plymouth and the reign of the *CSS Albemarle*. The Tuscarora Native American Indians were early inhabitants of this region and their influence can be found in the names of the communities along the Roanoke River. "Roanoke" itself means "river of death," and, historically, the river would flood miles of wooded bottomland after intense rainfalls, destroying anything in its path. Today, dams control that flooding, although water levels can still vary widely with the weather. The original mode of transportation on the Roanoke River was the dugout canoe, and evidence of these canoes has been found in Creswell, near Phelps Lake.

During the late 1990s a grassroots group partnered with The Nature Conservatory, The Conservation Fund, local governments, and several landowners to form the Roanoke River Partners (RRP), which established a watery trail called the Roanoke River Paddle Trail (RRPT). This grassroots group started from the interest several people had in paddling the Roanoke River, prompting the formation of an independent, nonprofit group of individuals and organizations to ensure the natural beauty of the Roanoke River, the Albemarle Sound, and the communities with ties to the river. One of the goals was to preserve the environment while opening up the waterway to the public. Through this partnership, RRP has helped community and regional entities to boost their economic viability, sustain the natural environmental beauty of the river and its communities, and promote a healthy lifestyle. Established in the same fashion as models in the Everglades and the Okefenokee Swamp, the RRPT offers a similar network of camping platforms but, unlike some of the other models, has very few portages.

The river and its black-water tributaries offer unique wilderness experiences—a 200-mile wilderness eco-adventure—for kayakers and canoeists as they traverse the largest intact bottomland hardwood swamp forest east of the Mississippi beneath towering hundred-year-growth cypress and tupelo trees. The area is home to more than 214 bird species, including 88 breeding species, of which 44 are neotropical migratory species. The most common avian neighbors along the Roanoke River are barred owls, wood ducks, herons, egrets, osprey, and bald eagles, but serious bird-watchers will visit to catch sight of the rare cerulean warbler or the Mississippi kite. Throughout this wilderness, the paddler may encounter black bears, bobcats, beavers, minks, white-tail deer, snakes, wild turkeys, and many other animals. The ecosystem also hosts a variety of fish, including striped bass, largemouth bass, black crappie, catfish, and gar. Depending on how far upstream the Albemarle Sound is being pushed in by winds or storms, saltwater fish can sometimes be found.

Currently, ten camping platforms stand along the RRPT, and plans for later development call for adding traditional dryland campsites, cabins, and perhaps even tree houses as lodging options for paddlers. The platforms, which are generally four feet above the swamp waters, are constructed in harmony with the environment. Some have boardwalks leading up to them as sites were chosen to have the least invasive impact on the area. Some decks are accessible by docking steps at staggered heights to allow for the fluctuation of the water level or boardwalks. All decks can accommodate a minimum of six paddlers and their tents comfortably, and innovative design allows campers to hang tarps or mosquito nets, lash down tents, or hang gear to dry. On the platform or boardwalk of each campsite is a privy with half-walls facing the wilderness so as not to obstruct one's view of the habitat. When construction is completed, a new double platform linked by walkways and a wood and steel cable swinging bridge will meet the needs of larger groups.

Roanoke River Partners operates the RRPT under the "Leave No Trace" guidelines. These encourage the traveler to plan ahead, be self-sufficient and self-contained, and respect wildlife and others. Travelers are counseled to leave the environment as they find it. Strong emphasis is placed on not marking trails; nonremoval of natural artifacts, rocks, or plants; and not adding any kind of foreign object to the natural environment. The theory of the campsite and trail is "pack in and pack out," meaning that paddlers are expected to contain all their waste and to generate as little gray water as possible. Small portable toilets are supplied upon registration (required) and then returned after completion of the trip. No campfires are allowed, but campers are permitted to carry in camp stoves. This is a wilderness area and campers/paddlers are expected to respect that fact.

The camping trail includes the communities along the Roanoke River as well. Roanoke River Partners defines its organizational goal as promoting ecotourism. As the use of the RRPT continues to grow, opportunities exist for the development of businesses along the route, whether directly associated with paddlers'/campers' needs or linked to trail activities. Several towns are experiencing a revitalization of their downtown districts as businesses spring up that are geared to the influx of ecotourists to the trail or other natural attractions in the area. Already a few businesses supply canoes or kayaks and camping goods and supplies, and RRP is working to encourage more. The towns located along the Roanoke River are seeing an increase in demand for food services and accommodations. Other beneficiaries of this enterprise are gasoline stations, museums, and historic sites.

The towns and communities are realizing an additional value: the population can expand as visitors along the Roanoke River find a connection to a rural lifestyle. One boat builder handcrafts wooden canoes and boats near the trail, and the market is ripe for the establishment of other types of outfitter and guiding businesses. Businesses for nonparticipants will also be needed. One potential growth area is historical venues as more people desire to tour destinations important to our past. In conjunction with the Civil War Trails Program, the town of Plymouth and Washington County have added four historic markers. Other locations along the RRPT that were important during this time of our country's history are in the process of gaining recognition and historic site designation. However, the most important outcome of all this activity is the impact on the local citizenry, who are excited and involved in the promotion of the Roanoke River Paddle Trail and recognize the economic benefits of this enterprise.

Chapter 8

Strategies for Sustainable Tourism

Big buildings belong in cities, not on the beach.

Jimmy Buffett, *Where Is Joe Merchant?*, 1993

TOURISM DEVELOPMENT MUST HAVE A STRATEGY

The key to sustainable tourism is to manage the destination effectively within a given natural, built, or cultural environment to provide benefits to the local population, to enrich the visit of the tourist, and to preserve the tourism products for future generations to enjoy. Natural areas must be preserved and flora and fauna protected. Customs and traditions must not be discarded and privacy and dignity must be maintained. Ultimately, sustainable tourism, properly managed, will add to the quality of life of the residents, visitors, and tourism employees alike. It is important to develop strategies and guidelines to ensure that this happens.

When sustainable tourism guidelines are contemplated, certain basic precepts should be kept in mind:

1. The first requisite is to inventory, assess, and seek to develop as many visitor attractions as possible that have roots in the local community or complement local activities. Local cultural and heritage initiatives, if properly developed and maintained, can improve the overall ambiance and cleanliness of the area and add to the quality of community life. At the same time, local pride in the area may evolve with good leadership as tourism moves throughout the community.

2. Development within each local community should strive to preserve the uniqueness of the environment. A community should capitalize on any period historical buildings, special natural re-

93

    sources, or sensitive culture traits available. This maintains the authenticity of the area, enriching its value to the visitors and local people alike.

3. Any realistic guidelines for sustainable tourism development must include community involvement. This is good public relations and is essential to the ultimate success of the endeavor. The community then becomes an effective force in the implementation of the program.

4. A local community should seek to measure tourism development in light of environmental and social costs and benefits to the area. Sustainable tourism should be viewed in terms of both short-term and long-term value to the community. Intangible values such as quality of life should be included in the overall quantification.

5. Marketing of sustainable tourism must utilize e-commerce tools as well as taking advantage of "coopetition" (partnerships, strategic alliances). Most sustainable tourism destinations will rely heavily on niche or other forms of database marketing. Effective, regularly updated Web sites will be key to marketing the local tourism products.

As a community, state/province, or region begins to develop a strategic plan, it is important to gather local and national statistics and research on the status and interest of travelers in sustainable tourism products. For example, in 2002, the Travel Industry Association of America conducted a landmark study (sponsored by *National Geographic Traveler*) that documented the strong positive feelings of U.S. travelers toward the preservation of the natural environment, history, and culture.

STRATEGIES FOR RURAL AREAS AS WELL

Agriculture has become more mechanized with increased productivity, timber production faces greater competition from foreign markets, and mineral resources are becoming scarcer. As mentioned in Chapter 7, economic planners in many rural areas of the world are looking for alternative products, services, and markets to replace their former reliance on agriculture, timber, mining, and certain manufacturing products. Many areas are looking toward more sustainable resources as a development tool, and tourism is a highly viable option because many of its products rely on an area's cultural, historic, ethnic, geographic, and natural uniqueness. Such product opportunities are increasingly being viewed as strategies for keeping rural communities economically viable.

In its 1991-1992 report on tourism, the OECD (Organisation for Economic Co-Operation and Development 1994) states that six factors determine the suitability of rural areas for tourism development:

1. Scenic value including mountains, seashores, lakes, islands, rivers, *and* special interest scenery such as wetlands or mixed deciduous forest
2. Special wildlife assets
3. Cultural assets including historic buildings, towns, villages, sites and/or ethnic heritage of all types
4. Special facilities for sports including hunting, fishing, skiing, and hiking
5. Ease of access by large populations
6. Effective promotional, commercial, and management skills

The OECD adds that these factors are not exclusive to rural areas, and that the possession of any one or all of them does not necessarily guarantee success. However, consideration of these factors can help some areas determine whether their sustainable tourism strategies warrant further discussion and planning.

Often rural populations live close to areas that can be utilized for sustainable tourism development. As sustainable tourism can, in some cases, represent a valid economic alternative for the local area, the inhabitants would have additional incentives to protect their natural environment. Also, because of their knowledge of the area, its history, and culture, local residents can be trained as guides, work in other local tourism services, including accommodations and restaurants, or own their own tourism-related businesses.

Some rural areas have been highly successful in developing significant heritage and cultural activities, special events, festivals, or services relating to history and heritage into sustainable tourism products. This may be as simple as creating or restoring special local celebrations of past events—for example, the Trade Days Festival in Johnson County, northeast Tennessee, where communities reenact the eighteenth-century trading activities between Native American tribes in the area and the local settlers. This is now an annual three-day festival with special events, including demonstrations of a moonshine still, winemaking, tobacco twisting, cheese making, churning, apple butter making, spinning, and weaving and wool carding. One of the most successful components of the festival (of particular interest to international visitors) has been the Native American powwow. The aim for such activities should be to

- generate new business;
- encourage repeat business;
- increase customer lengths of stay;
- increase customer spending;
- promote the use of facilities during off-peak periods;
- increase customer satisfaction; and
- create new products that will appeal to new target market segments.

The return on investment can be substantially higher from effective programming of special events than from expansion of facilities. A rural area can develop hundreds of event and festival opportunities to help market new products.

PRACTICAL GUIDELINES FOR SUSTAINABLE TOURISM

Carefully planned sustainable tourism can fulfill economic, environmental, and social goals while maintaining cultural integrity and an ecological balance. However, it also involves making hard political choices based on complex social, economic, and environmental tradeoffs. It requires a broader, longer-term vision than that traditionally used in community planning and decision making. A planner attempting to incorporate this broader vision into local policies and practices can use the basic guidelines from "An Action Strategy for Sustainable Tourism Development" from the "Globe '90 Conference" in Vancouver, BC, Canada (Globe '90, Tourism Stream Action Strategy Committee 1990).

Throughout all stages of tourism development and operation, a careful assessment, monitoring, and mediation program should be in place to allow the local people the opportunity to respond to changes and make adjustments. It is helpful to have an experienced "outside" expert in the planning process, but ultimately it is the local community that must agree on the process and implement the plan. It takes commitment, perseverance, and patience throughout the process.

The following are some practical guidelines taken from *Ecotourism: The Potentials and Pitfalls* (Boo 1990) for a local planner to apply to a new product with nature tourism or ecotourism attributes. Nature tourists can be people casually walking through an undisturbed forest, or scuba divers admiring coral formations, or birdwatchers adding birds to their lists. Nature tourism is a special segment of the market that must be especially responsive to environmental issues. These guidelines encourage the community and tourism constituencies to work together toward a common sustainable tourism goal

- The success of nature tourism depends on the conservation of nature. Many parks are threatened, and it is critical for everyone involved with nature tourism to realize that intact natural resources are the foundation of the product.
- Nature tourism sites need revenue for protection and maintenance, much of which can be generated directly from entry fees and sales of products. Many protected areas charge nominal or no entrance fees and provide few if any auxiliary services. Nature tourists also desire gift shops, food services, and lodging facilities and expect to pay for them.
- Tourists are a valuable audience for environmental education. In many parks, opportunities are missed to provide environmental education. Whether "hardcore" nature tourists or "new" visitors with little background in natural history, all tourists can enhance their appreciation of the area through information brochures, exhibits and guides.
- Nature tourism will contribute to rural development when local residents are brought into the planning process. For nature tourism to be a tool for conservation and rural development, a concerted effort must be made to incorporate local populations into development of the tourism industry. In some cases, tourism to

protect areas is not benefiting the surrounding population because they are not involved.

- Opportunities are emerging for new relationships between con-
servationists and tour operators. Traditionally, these groups have
not worked together; often they have been in direct opposition.
However, as more tourists come to parks and reserves, tour operators have the opportunity to become more actively involved
with the conservation of these areas through education for their
clientele and donations to park management.[1]

BEST PRACTICES FOR SUSTAINABLE TOURISM

To realize the potential opportunities offered by sustainable tourism, it is important that local communities and businesses have goals
and objectives to chart the way. Some guidelines and principles have
already been discussed that apply equally to the natural and built environments, ecological and cultural programs, and education and interpretation of areas visited. The strategy is to develop an integrated
approach to tourism planning and infrastructure. The overall objective is to have an environmentally and culturally sustainable tourism
development program that will allow the tourism industry to be competitive and local communities to be economically viable. Environmentally sound tourism best practices will preserve the environment
and educate visitors.

I have mentioned already that some organizations, government entities, and private sector groups have gotten the message and are beginning to understand the long-term benefits of managing sustainable
tourism. In 2004, for example, a dozen or so conferences focused on
best practices for sustainable tourism development, and more were
scheduled for 2005. Although governments at all levels across the
globe have been slow to endorse strong sustainable tourism management programs, they are increasingly coming on board as they begin
to understand the economic, environmental, and social benefits. Some
private sector companies have become better educated about sustainable tourism, and they see both the public relations value of supporting sustainable tourism management and the resulting bottom-line
growth. The not-for-profit organizations have a better track record of
endorsement, but this is not surprising and it is not across the board.

For example, our educational institutions have generally been slow to adopt sustainable tourism initiatives in their programs. The only university tourism center in the United States that has "sustainable tourism" in its title appears to be the Center for Sustainable Tourism at the University of Colorado at Boulder. East Carolina University in Greenville, North Carolina, is carefully investigating the "management of sustainable tourism," but it remains to be seen what will happen more generally in the educational process at university level. It will take a lot of effort by many people and organizations to arrive at the level of excellence in managing sustainable tourism advocated by this book.

Alongside sustainable tourism's numerous success stories are many failures. The National Lewis and Clark Bicentennial Commemoration 2004-2006, which had the opportunity to be a great success, has thus far received mixed reviews. Millions of dollars have been spent on infrastructure, whereas almost no funding has been devoted to providing assistance to rural communities along the trail to develop marketing and promotional strategies or to incorporate specific sustainable tourism programs. The program seems to be relying on the concept of "build it and they will come" instead of "build it, sustain it, and effectively market it and they will come and have a quality experience." Many other examples can be cited of potential sustainable tourism projects without a strategic tourism plan to chart the appropriate course of action for their ultimate success.

The case study of the Tallgrass Prairie National Preserve in the Flint Hills of Kansas illustrates an attempt to incorporate best practices for sustainable tourism development. The preserve is a "work in progress" example of many of the ideas discussed in this chapter. The fact that it was finally approved as a national park and that it is a cooperative effort by a national government, a nonprofit organization, and other partners makes it a classic case study for sustainable tourism. The real challenge for this park is to achieve better support, publicity, and marketing, and inclusion in the mainstream of activities for the area, state, and nation. The national parks are already under considerable pressure in terms of their maintenance and management: the popular parks are overcrowded and hard to manage; the less visited parks are often underutilized but still require good maintenance. It is difficult to balance all the pieces of the park management process to achieve both a quality tourism experience and sustainability.

CASE STUDY: A RURAL MASTERPIECE—
KANSAS TALLGRASS PRAIRIE NATIONAL PRESERVE

The Tallgrass Prairie National Preserve brochure begins as follows: "Whether you are visiting from the next county, a distant state, or another country, you now have a prairie destination, rich in the unique history, culture, and ecology of the Great Plains."[2] From the *Kansas City Star* ("Newest U.S. Park Is Prairie Land," June 1, 1997): "America's newest national park doesn't have towering forests, majestic rock formations or mountain lakes. It does have a big sky and rolling acres of prairie grass that bend as wind gusts race along the flat landscape." The National Park Trust and the National Park Service dedicated the Tallgrass Prairie National Preserve in the scenic Flint Hills of central Kansas on May 31, 1997.

At one time nearly 400,000 square miles of tallgrass prairie stretched from Ohio to the Rocky Mountains and from Canada to Texas. Less than 4 percent of that prairie remains today, much of it in the rolling Flint Hills, which look like giant grass-covered ocean swells and have become home to the first national park dedicated to the tallgrass prairie and the people who lived on it.

Capturing the history and heritage of the tallgrass into a national park system demonstrates the creative effort and persistence of a few dedicated people and a national organization, the National Park Trust. For more than forty years there had been an interest in preserving the rich natural and cultural past by setting aside land for prairie tallgrass. The Flint Hills were a natural site for such an effort and for studying the rich history of Native American cultures and the pioneer spirit of America. The question was how to make it happen.

Some of the impetus for "sustaining" the prairie tallgrass for future generations might have come from such popular books as *Little House on the Prairie* by Laura Ingalls Wilder (1935/2004) and *PrairyErth* by William Least Heat-Moon (1991). Most important were the availability of a large area, regional involvement, political backing, strong advocates, and widespread support for such a project. Fortunately, all these ingredients existed.

The Z Bar/Spring Hill Ranch, located two miles north of Strong City in Chase County, Kansas, in the Flint Hills area is a near-perfect site for preserving prairie tallgrass. It has a rich ranching history, covers about 10,894 acres, and has several well-kept historical buildings.

When Stephen F. Jones built his home on the ranch in the early 1880s, it was the crowning achievement in his career as a cattleman. Built with hand-cut native limestone, the eleven-room house is characteristic of the Second Empire style of nineteenth-century architecture. The massive three-story barn is impressive in its own right. Visitors also enjoy seeing the Lower Fox Creek School, a one-room schoolhouse located on a nearby hilltop. A spring on the hillside provided water to the house, hence the name, the Spring Hill Ranch. The ranch was designated a National Historic Landmark in February 1997, and several buildings on the ranch are listed on the National Register of Historic Places. The entire preserve is now a National Historic Landmark.

The concept of a sustainable tallgrass prairie preserve in its present form dates from July 1988, when the National Audubon Society acquired an option to purchase the Z Bar/Spring Hill Ranch. The Audubon Society suggested the property be purchased and designated a unit of the National Park System. In spite of their diverse views, in 1989 a group of Chase County citizens formed the Flint Hills National Monument Committee, which proposed the ranch be designated the Flint Hills Prairie National Monument. The National Park Service agreed to conduct a study on this proposal, and in January 1990 a study team was organized and work on the project began.

By March 1991, the study was completed, concluding that the ranch contained significant natural and cultural resources, making it both suitable and feasible as a potential addition to the National Park System. The property clearly fit the mold for sustainable tourism.

Based on the study and other information, the National Park Trust (a not-for-profit organization) purchased the ranch site and began generating public support for the project through education programs, open houses, tours, and special events. Meanwhile, political moves by the Kansas Congressional Delegation were in high gear to get the Z Bar Ranch designated as part of the National Park System. On November 12, 1996, Public Law 104-333, the Tallgrass Prairie National Preserve Act of 1996, was enacted and the newest national park was established. Today, the National Park Trust and the National Park Service coordinate efforts to preserve this remnant of the ancient prairie that once blanketed much of central North America. As new plans for the preserve evolve, one important current need is for some innovative measures to promote it to potential visitors.

The preserve, once the hunting grounds for the Kansa and Osage Indians, contains hills and prairie streams that are home to a wide variety of life. This incredible ecosystem hosts 400 species of plants, 150 kinds of birds, 29 types of reptiles and amphibians, and 39 species of mammals. The prairie flora and fauna, along with the historic buildings, the Native American cultural history, and the rich legacy of ranching, are all preserved for present and future generations to enjoy. The preserve is a model for public/private partnerships in sustainable tourism; the federal government (National Park Service) and a nonprofit organization (National Park Trust) are cooperatively managing the park along with numerous state, private, and community partners to preserve America's prairie heritage.

Chapter 9

Managing Sustainable Tourism

A guest never forgets the host who had treated him kindly.

Homer, *The Odyssey,* ninth century BC

A PARADIGM SHIFT

Since the new millennium began, there have been more conferences, more studies, and more efforts at defining and implementing sustainable tourism activities than during the entire twentieth century. Sustainable tourism is a very positive response in an industry that sometimes ignores any venture that does not have immediate dollar signs to invigorate its development. Many communities are beginning to realize that if they manage tourism well, they can reap the economic rewards, conserve the environment, and improve social conditions. This paradigm shift toward careful management of sustainable tourism needs to be well understood if we are to leave a positive tourism legacy for future generations. As the previous chapters and many of the case studies suggest, it might be appropriate at this stage to dissect the critical needs of the local community into three parts: economic, environmental, and social.

Most communities and business entities look at the potential economic returns on their investments before they get too excited about sustainable tourism development, marketing, and promotion. As mentioned in Chapter 1, in the 1970s most tourism projects included, at the outset, an economic impact statement. Any major community or business initiative for a tourism activity was looked at primarily as an economic development tool that could ultimately yield a positive economic return on the investment. Questions revolved around how many new jobs would be created, whether additional income would be generated, new businesses spawned, or new products developed, and whether the project would result in more economic diversification and integration for the community and tax benefits. These economic concerns were usually considered before other impacts, such as the impact of the project on the environment.

By the 1980s, changes were afoot. Communities, states/provinces, and countries began to be more concerned about the environment, eventually leading to global environmental conferences that included major segments devoted to the impact of tourism on the environment. One result was that an environmental impact statement as well as an economic impact statement had to be prepared for major project developments. Destinations aimed increasingly to be referred to as "green." Europe was one of the leaders, with new guidelines for tourism development that reflected a need and desire to protect the environment and conserve resources (OECD 1994). Most international bodies with an interest in tourism, such as the World Tourism Organization, the Organisation for Economic Co-Operation and Development, the Organization of American States, Asia-Pacific Economic Cooperation, and the Caribbean Tourism Organization, were espousing new doctrine stressing the need to be more concerned about the environment and new ways of marketing "environmental tourism."

The 1990s saw another shift in tourism development. It became more fashionable to talk about the social impact of tourism—in other words, whether tourism development was adding to the quality of life of the local citizens. Part of quality of life was the positive impact that tourism could have on the natural environment (ecotourism, agritourism, rural tourism) and the built environment (history, heritage, art, and culture). Even though a project is economically viable or environmentally sound, it might not necessarily improve the quality of life of most members of the community. Gradually, any new tourism development project had not only to "pass muster" in terms of its economic and environmental impact, but also to include a social impact statement.

In the new millennium many tourism leaders see the management of sustainable tourism as a mechanism that ties economic, environmental, and social issues together into a single management philosophy. If the destination is managed correctly, it can be marketed and promoted better. Through database marketing, e-commerce tools, and special Web sites, it becomes possible to find just the right niche market that fits a sustainable tourism product. By managing the development, marketing, and promotion of sustainable tourism through a strategic sustainable tourism plan, the community is able to project itself as a very special place that tourists will want to visit, return to, and possibly even retire to.

RECOGNIZE AND PLAN STRATEGY

Often an area that receives large numbers of visitors or is heavily dependent on tourism does not see the signs of overdevelopment or tourism saturation until it is too late. Thus, tourism areas with large visitor numbers need constantly to monitor the impact of intense demand on the natural and built environment and on their social and cultural values. In effect, the sustainability of an area is its ability to maintain the quality of its physical, social, cultural, and environmental resources while it competes in the marketplace. The following warning signals apply:

- Erosion of the natural environment as a result of overdevelopment or overintensive uses
- Pollution of ocean, lake, and river environments through boating, littering, or other tourism-related activities
- Visual, noise, and air pollution from overdevelopment (hotels blocking scenic views), tourism traffic (transportation or built congestion), or unregulated air quality (smokestacks, emissions)
- Utility shortages caused by overuse or capacity limitation during peak visitation or according to time-of-day usage (particularly electricity, sewage, and water usage)
- Traffic congestion at airports, roadways, and tourist sites during high tourism season (or because of a lack of adequate facilities)
- Lack of public facilities (restrooms, trash disposal, parking)
- Inadequate attention to the safety and security needs of visitors
- Friction and resentment between the host community and tourists
- Social problems, including general crime, drug abuse, and prostitution
- Overcrowding and damage to national shrines, monuments, and historical structures

It is important to look at how we prevent such problems, which already exist in many parts of the world, and provide for sustainable tourism development, at what point saturation will be reached, and what kinds of creative management plans need to be developed.

In addition, a local community must be prepared for the costs involved in providing quality tourism benefits, for example:

- Can the community adequately finance the development and maintenance of the tourism destination and products?
- Does the community have the infrastructure and facilities to support its tourism projects and programs?
- Will tourism add to the quality of life of the local community?
- Is the community ready to provide for the promotion and marketing of the area?
- Should the community look beyond domestic tourism promotion and evaluate its ability to attract international visitors as well?
- What does the community provide in terms of technical assistance, education, and skills development?
- Has the community prepared economic, environmental, and social impact statements for its tourism development projects?
- How will the community deal with the regulatory issues for its tourism development?
- Where does the community go for expert help in developing its tourism projects and programs?

Answers to some of these questions must be found almost at the beginning of the development phase of the project. If they are ignored, such issues could prove detrimental to the long-term success of a perfectly valid opportunity for tourism. Sometimes, an outside consultant, university staff, or state tourism office staff can help communities avoid these obstacles to success.

In the popular book *Tourism: Principles, Practices, and Philosophies,* the authors Charles Goeldner and J. R. Brent Ritchie (2003) very succinctly explain why sustainable tourism development needs a strategic plan:

1. All the stakeholders in tourism development should safeguard the natural environment with a view to achieving sound, continuous, and sustainable economic growth geared to satisfying eq-

uitably the needs and aspirations of present and future generations.

2. All forms of tourism development that are conducive to saving rare and precious resources, in particular water and energy, as well as avoiding so far as possible waste production, should be given priority and encouraged by national, regional, and local public authorities.

3. The staggering in time and space of tourist and visitor flows, particularly those resulting from paid leave and school holidays, and a more even distribution of holidays should be sought so as to reduce the pressure of tourism activity on the environment and enhance its beneficial impact on the tourism industry and the local economy.

4. Tourism infrastructure should be designed and tourism activities programmed in such a way as to protect the natural heritage composed of ecosystems and biodiversity and to preserve endangered species of wildlife. The stakeholders in tourism development, and especially professionals, should agree to the imposition of limitations or constraints on their activities when these are exercised in particularly sensitive areas—desert, polar, or high mountain regions, coastal areas, tropical forest or wetlands propitious to the creation of nature reserves or protected areas.

5. Nature tourism and ecotourism are recognized as being particularly conducive to enriching and enhancing the standing of tourism, provided they respect the natural heritage and local populations and are in keeping with the carrying capacity of the sites. (p. 430)

The authors pay special attention to the sustainable attributes of "cultural heritage":

1. Tourism resources belong to the common heritage of mankind. The communities in whose territories they are situated have particular rights and obligations to them.

2. Tourism policies and activities should be conducted with respect for the artistic, archaeological, and cultural heritage, which they should protect and pass on to future generations. Particular care should be devoted to preserving and upgrading monuments, shrines, and museums as well as archaeological and his-

toric sites, which must be widely open to tourist visits. Encouragement should be given to public access to privately owned cultural property and monuments, with respect for the rights of their owners, as well as to religious buildings, without prejudice to normal needs of worship.

3. Financial resources derived from visits to cultural sites and monuments should, at least, be used for the upkeep, safeguarding, development, and embellishment of this heritage.

4. Tourism activity should be planned in such a way as to allow traditional cultural products, crafts, and folklore to survive and flourish, rather than causing them to degenerate and become standardized. (p. 431)

DON'T GET TOO CROWDED

As already discussed, a successful sustainable tourism strategy should seek to maximize the developmental benefits of tourism while preserving and enhancing the natural, built, and cultural environments on which it depends. Any business plan for resort development should identify, from the beginning, a set of guidelines or standards that determine the carrying capacity of the project, which depends on the project, area, available transportation, and other factors. Fundamentally, carrying capacity relates to the available infrastructure being able to absorb the tourist traffic. Many problems arise because too many people live in or visit a fragile environment, which includes the ecology of the area, the flora and fauna, monuments and cultural facilities, public utilities, historic buildings, and heritage resources. When the visitor and host population are both experiencing exceptionally crowded conditions, the upper limits of the carrying capacity have been passed, the negative effects of tourism become apparent, and the quality of the environment and the tourism product begins to decline for both residents and visitors.

The key, of course, is to have built-in parameters that signal early on that an area is beginning to reach its carrying capacity. Otherwise, it is likely the local population will no longer welcome visitors and tourists will no longer have a quality experience. The managers of sustainable tourism development projects should seek to promote, establish, and implement a strategy and a program of concerted actions designed to ensure a balance between the visitors, the host popula-tion, and the environment so as not to exceed the carrying capacity.

Carrying capacity has become a major concern for some popular national parks, tourism destinations, and outdoor recreation areas. On certain holidays, such as Memorial Day and Labor Day in the United States, many wonderful tourism sites exceed their carrying capacity, creating not only travel congestion, but also negative impacts on the destination itself. Similarly, many parts of Europe suffer from over-use of facilities during the popular travel month of August. In many of the Caribbean countries and in certain high-density locations in the United States, Europe, and elsewhere, we are seeing a lower-quality tourism experience for many visitors and the likelihood that future generations will not be able to enjoy certain popular tourism products at all. This is a critical situation that needs to be addressed by sustainable tourism management.

The case study on Banff National Park at the end of this chapter is an excellent example of the recognition of carrying capacity con-cerns. Without the foresight of many individuals and agencies, much of the appeal and splendor of Banff National Park would have been lost. The park, already a quality tourism destination, can now set in motion its plan to ensure its future sustainability.

Costa Rica is another good example. This small Central American country has one of the finest ecotourism programs in the world. Al-though economic development is critical for the country, Costa Rica also recognizes the importance of balanced tourism, in terms of num-bers of tourists and the capacity of the destination. For the most part, Costa Ricans have used ecotourism in the best way possible—to pre-serve the land and select activities to enhance and appreciate the natu-ral beauty and culture of the place; in exchange for help in conserving the land, citizens have been provided with economic benefits, includ-ing jobs, to supplement farming income.

EFFECTIVE MANAGEMENT IS THE WAY TO GO

Management strategies to combat problems are emerging. Solu-tions are sometimes long term, expensive, and disruptive to the tour-ism industry. However, management approaches of a practical nature are worth considering in a sustainable tourism development program.

The OAS (Organization of American States 1995) publication "Sustainable Nature and Heritage Tourism Development: A Summary of OAS Technical Assistance in the Caribbean" suggests changed roles for the public and private sectors in sustainable tourism development. Two fundamental elements of this change are (1) that participants, or "players," must form cooperative partnerships to achieve successful sustainability and (2) that these partnerships must include all those who will be affected by the development. In one sense, the new and expanded roles of the private sector and the community counterbalance the reduced role of government, especially in day-to-day implementation and operation activities. Yet privatization in sustainable tourism development does not mean that government takes a back seat to the other players; nor does it mean that the government should no longer apply protective standards in the development process. On the contrary, one of the key roles of government in sustainable tourism development is to bring responsible people together and elicit their input into planning and management decisions. Another strategy is to apply innovative technology to achieve sustainable tourism, as in the case of Maho Bay, where technology that minimizes waste and maximizes the effective use of resources such as energy, water, and construction materials was utilized (see the case study at the end of Chapter 10). To be effective, this technology must demonstrably increase economic benefits. Developmental, educational, and awareness programs to inform the public and visitors about the importance of protected areas, conservation principles, and the need to respect fragile environments can also be helpful. Here, the media can contribute toward spreading the word about specific sites, and grade school, high school, and university programs can educate people about the sustainable use of resources.

The Good Earthkeeping Program sponsored by the American Hotel and Lodging Association in cooperation with the U.S. Environmental Protection Agency to encourage hotel and motel guests to conserve water is one of many cooperative programs. The sponsors have developed a colorful laminated water conservation brochure in five languages (English, French, Spanish, German, and Japanese) for distribution to hotel guests in their rooms. The brochure briefly mentions that only 3 percent of the earth's water is fresh and that one way to conserve water is not to wash bed linens daily. The polite message is as follows: "If you would like to participate [this portion in red lettering], please leave this card on the pillow and we will remake your bed, but not change your bed linens. Otherwise, we will gladly change your linens daily."

The good news is that more and more countries, communities, and companies are recognizing that through good management practices, considerable progress toward sustainable tourism can be made. Countries such as Australia, the Bahamas, Bermuda, Canada, Costa Rica, The Netherlands, New Zealand, and Switzerland made outstanding progress in the 1990s toward recognizing and putting into effect programs in sustainable tourism. At the same time, organizations such as the World Travel and Tourism Council and the World Tourism Organization have sponsored programs to encourage private tourism businesses to practice sustainable tourism management.

Canada has one of the finest examples of good management principles in Banff National Park, which is the case study for this chapter. This park, more than any other I have researched, embodies what quality management can mean in terms of sustainable tourism. It saw the paradigm shift coming and adjusted accordingly. It recognized the issue of carrying capacity and took action to counter the negative consequences. Finally, it attempted to reduce problems through effective management.[1]

CASE STUDY: THE EMBODIMENT OF MANAGED TOURISM— CANADA, BANFF NATIONAL PARK

Canada has led the way in managing environmental activities in parks and has devised practical tools for tourism development. Many facets of Canada's leadership role can be observed throughout thirty-eight national parks maintained by the Canadian Parks System. Much of what Canada has already accomplished is transferable to the management of sustainable tourism beyond the park system. Canada's National Parks Act of 1930 states, "The Parks are dedicated to the people of Canada for their benefit, education, and enjoyment. . . . such parks shall be maintained and made use of so as to leave them unimpaired for the enjoyment of future generations." The first amendments to this impressive act, in 1988, emphasize ecological integrity and the protection of "intact ecosystems," and include public participation in management. More recently, in 1994, additional enhancements were made to the "Guiding Principles and Operational Policies" to further protect the environment on the basis "that park management must reflect Canada's national identity and its international responsibilities." One of the finest applications of good management aimed toward positive concepts of sustainable tourism can be found in Banff National Park.

Banff, which was established in 1885 in the Rocky Mountains in Alberta Province west of Calgary, is Canada's first and best-known national park. The park has superb scenery and outstanding recreational opportunities that attract millions of people from many different countries. As a UN World Heritage Site, Banff National Park must meet the highest standards of environmental stewardship.

A small community of 7,600 people lives within the bounds of the park, carrying on normal everyday activities. Banff is a very special experiment in blending community life, tourist visits, and related activities in a historic and natural environment. Constant efforts are made to strengthen the ecological integrity of the park and achieve a balance between conservation and use. This is important, as forecasts suggest 19 million visitors by 2020 (Banff National Park 1996, p. 4). In the "Banff National Park Management Plan Summary," the Minister of Canadian Heritage calls the park "a place where nature will always be the integral part of everyone's visit, responsibility and lives" (Minister of Public Works and Government Services Canada 1997, p. 4). The minister goes on to say that the plan is the blueprint for action into the twenty-first century and that "[t]his vision could be a model for all our parks, for generations to come." The Minister's direction for Banff has six themes:

1. A place for nature
2. A place for visitors
3. A place for community
4. A place for heritage tourism
5. A place for open management
6. A place for environmental stewardship

These themes, which are elaborated on in the plan, are the essence of managing sustainable tourism. For example, the section on "A place for heritage tourism" includes the following:

Banff National Park must be a place where the protected heritage environment is an integral part of everyone's visit, where businesses and services enhance the visitor's appreciation of this special place.

- Tourism plays a key role in presenting the very best of Canada. Private sector services are essential to enable millions of visitors to experience and learn about the Park. Tourism will continue to contribute more than $700 million annually to the local and regional economies and to generate 18,000 jobs.
- The Minister calls upon the tourism industry to develop a heritage tourism strategy that builds upon the ideas of the Task Force and addresses issues of service levels and appropriateness and to adopt the Code of Ethics and Guidelines for Sustainable Tourism.
- The Minister's direction emphasizes expanding on the opportunities that enable visitors to experience and learn about the Park.

The current management plan for Banff National Park, approved in 1997, is a fifteen-year "dynamic" plan. In accordance with the Canada National Parks Act, the plan is publicly reviewed and amended, as appropriate, every five years. This process helps to ensure that Banff National Park remains a quality destination for future generations to enjoy.

The plan makes it clear that Banff National Park is, first and foremost, a place for nature. Ecological integrity is its cornerstone and is key to its future. The plan also recognizes that the park is a place for people and for heritage tourism (which by Canada's definition includes natural history, human heritage, arts, philosophy, and institutions). Banff National Park combines the rugged beauty of the Rocky Mountains and the splendor of a pristine environment. Its preservation of history, culture, flora, and fauna offers an environment for visitors' enjoyment and educational opportunities. Banff's popularity, its ecological and cultural importance, its contribution to the economy, and its services to visitors all serve to create a park that is quite unlike any other protected area in Canada. Not every aspect of the plan is adhered to, and problems arise from time to time, but the park is an example of future directions in sustainable tourism. It takes constant vigilance, excellent management, and governmental foresight to maintain this park as a world model for managing sustainable tourism.

Chapter 10

More to Say About the Future

Travel and change of place impart new vigor to the mind.

Lucius Annaeus Seneca, *De tranquillitate animi,* ca. AD 60

INVENTORY, ASSESS, PLAN, DEVELOP, MARKET, AND MANAGE

An interesting Asia-Pacific Economic Cooperation (APEC) Sec-retariat study, "Environmentally Sustainable Tourism in APEC Member Economies," draws some interesting conclusions that can be applied more widely (APEC Secretariat 1996). To paraphrase the report, it is clear that properly managed sustainable tourism can lead not only to economic and environmental (built and natural) benefits, but also to the peace of mind that sites of historical significance, traditional culture, and native species will be available for this and future generations to appreciate. The report goes on to say, "These benefits are not cost-free. In fact, they will not be available in the long run unless society recognizes the value of natural and cultural resources, manages their use, and charges appropriately for their use and protection" (p. vi). It recommends attention to planning and management as key to sustainable tourism. The environment, history, heritage, traditions, and culture are a major part of tourism, and they must be preserved and enhanced to sustain tourism for the future. The report goes on to say that "well-planned and managed tourism can provide economic benefits to an economy as a whole, provide better employment and living standards for local residents, and maintain or even improve the quality of the local environment" (pp. 1-4). Although the roles of governments and the private sector may vary from place to place, along with the ways of financing these activities considered acceptable, both remain essential agents of environmentally sustainable tourism, which ultimately offers APEC member economies a strong mechanism of growth, while preserving natural, cultural, and historical resources.

If the planning and management of the historic, cultural, and natural resources are approached properly, the quality and integrity of the setting, whether natural or cultural, will become an integral part of tourism. Although much of the responsibility for preserving this legacy rests with the private and public sectors, the visitor also has responsibilities. A good example of such responsibilities is contained in a "Code of Ethics and Guidelines for Sustainable Tourism," Tourism Industry Association of Canada:

1. Enjoy our diverse natural and cultural heritage and help us to protect and preserve it.
2. Assist us in our conservation efforts through the efficient use of resources including energy and water.
3. Experience the friendliness of our people and the welcoming spirit of our communities. Help us to preserve these attributes by respecting our traditions, customs and local regulations.
4. Avoid activities which threaten wildlife or plant population, or which may be potentially damaging to our natural environment.
5. Select tourism products and services, which demonstrate social, cultural and environmental sensitivity.

Such good advice will lead to a high-quality tourism experience and should be included as part of the overall management and education plan of sustainable tourism.

Other efforts are under way to better plan and market well-managed sustainable tourism programs around the globe. As more countries recognize the advantages of tourism as a tool for trade, economic development, and international relations, governments and the private sector will face even greater pressure to provide quality tourism programs. The world is also beginning better to understand the impact of outside influences on tourism. For example, as a result of the terrorist attack on September 11, 2001, travel safety and security emerged as the world's number one tourism issue, resulting in airport security changes, border inspections, and additional identification measures. The Iraq war in 2003 demonstrated the corollary of the old cliché "When peace prevails, tourism flourishes." The effect of this war continues into 2005: people do not travel as much internationally during a major conflict. Also in 2003 came severe acute respiratory syndrome (SARS), a health issue that temporarily closed down tourism to certain destinations. Much of the world suffered an economic crisis in 2001-2004. At the end of 2004 and into 2005, the devastating tsunami and its aftermath in Southeast Asia caused unprecedented loss of life and damage. All these developments, along with smaller, individual country disasters, have had a detrimental impact on tourism, demonstrating just how vulnerable tourism is to world events and natural catastrophes. Add to these concerns the issue of "managing sustainable tourism" in a global context, and it is easy to see the reason for occasional reluctance or delay in taking action. Tourism will continue to grow despite difficult local or global circumstances. If we can plan and manage sustainable tourism growth to some extent, the world will have a greater opportunity for providing today's travelers and tomorrow's tourists with a quality tourism experience.

A GLOBAL SUSTAINABLE TOURISM INITIATIVE THAT MIGHT JUST WORK

As mentioned in Chapter 1, in October 1995, a new global initiative in sustainable tourism was launched in London as "Agenda 21 for the Travel and Tourism Industry: Toward Environmentally Sustainable Development." It was a joint effort by the World Travel and Tourism Council, the World Tourism Organization, and the Earth Council to create greater global interest in better management of sustainable tourism. Much of the impetus came from the 1992 Rio Earth Summit.

These three organizations sought international exposure and acceptance of the "Agenda 21" action plan as a systematic framework to encourage governments and businesses to make the tourism industry more environmentally responsible. The plan includes nine priority areas for government involvement in sustainable tourism:

1. Assessing the capacity of the existing regulatory, economic, and voluntary framework to bring about sustainable tourism

2. Assessing the economic, social, cultural, and environmental implications of the organization's operations
3. Training, education, and public awareness
4. Planning for sustainable tourism development
5. Facilitating the exchange of information, skills, and technology relating to sustainable tourism between developed and developing countries
6. Providing for the participation of all sectors of society
7. Designing new tourism products with sustainability at their core
8. Measuring progress in achieving sustainable development
9. Creating partnerships for sustainable development

These priority areas fit tourism development at the local, state/province, regional, national, and international levels. Since 1995, the World Tourism Organization has modified its sustainable tourism definition to match new trends in the industry. Sustainability principles refer to the environmental, economic, and sociocultural aspects of tourism development, and a suitable balance must be established between these three dimensions to guarantee long-term sustainability. Thus, according to the World Tourism Organization, managing sustainable tourism should also include the following principles:

1. Make optimal use of environmental resources that constitute a key element in tourism development, maintaining essential ecological processes and helping to conserve natural heritage and biodiversity.
2. Respect the sociocultural authenticity of host communities, conserve their built and living cultural heritage and traditional values, and contribute to intercultural understanding and tolerance.
3. Ensure viable, long-term economic operations that provide fairly distributed socioeconomic benefits to all stakeholders (including stable employment and income-earning opportunities, and social services to host communities) and contribute to poverty alleviation.

This effort, along with the efforts of other international organizations, helps guide the development process toward responsibly managed tourism.

Sustainable tourism development requires the informed participation of all relevant stakeholders, as well as strong political leadership to ensure wide participation and consensus building. Achieving sustainable tourism is a continuous process, and it requires constant monitoring of impacts, introducing preventive and corrective measures whenever necessary. Sustainable tourism should also maintain a high level of meaningful tourist satisfaction, raising awareness of sustainability issues and promoting sustainable tourism practices.

The World Travel and Tourism Council has also added to "Agenda 21" stronger prescriptions for tourism and the environment:

- Travel and tourism are integral to modern societies.
- Global awareness of environmental damage is developing rapidly.
- The resources of the world's largest industry can and must be harnessed to achieve environmental goals.
- The industry has the potential to influence billions of customers per year and to use its leverage to achieve beneficial environmental effects.
- Customers will exert growing pressure to achieve environmental improvements.
- Environmental lobbies will add pressure to develop good environmental practice.
- Self-regulation must be put in place rapidly and effectively and used to influence the development of appropriate and workable regulations.
- Corporate environmental mission statements are a vital first step toward self-regulation.
- Environmental leadership must come from the major international companies.

As mentioned in Chapters 2 and 3, Business Enterprises for Sustainable Travel (BEST) has formed partnerships with other organizations (including many of those named in this book), tourism destinations, tourism providers, educational institutions, and countries to make the travel community aware of the need to manage sustainable tourism. BEST holds meetings, seminars, and conferences to get many of the experts and organizations together to craft innovative and creative initiatives to perpetuate the benefits of sustainable tourism. One of the new entities joining in these meetings is the sustainable tourism office established by the National Geographic Society in

2003 and already working hard to gain attention for sustainable tourism destinations (for example, through its rating of 115 global destinations; Tourtellot 2004). The reputation of the National Geographic Society for quality publishing puts it in an excellent position to provide good publicity for sustainable tourism and to support quality tourism efforts.

RESEARCH AND EDUCATION—
OUR PATHWAY TO THE FUTURE

Since the "Agenda 21" initiative in 1995, interest in sustainable tourism has grown enormously. The University of Colorado at Boulder established the first Center for Sustainable Tourism in the United States in 1998. In 2001, Business Enterprises for Sustainable Travel was established in New York. By 2002, the University of the West Indies was making progress in sustainable tourism programs. In 2003 the National Geographic Society added a Director of Sustainable Tourism to its staff. In 2005 East Carolina University established an Institute for Tourism that includes "sustainable tourism" in its portfolio. Many educational and responsible institutions around the world now include sustainable tourism in their programs.

Future success in managing sustainable tourism will depend in part on training, education, and public awareness. The record for the proper management of sustainable tourism resources has not necessarily been a good one, and it will not improve unless the tourism community and the public at large are made aware of current positive and negative examples.

The training of students, academics, and managers in sustainable tourism is just beginning. We need now to identify the major issues and discuss them thoroughly in many different tourism venues. Educational institutions should add courses to explain the various forms of sustainable tourism and develop research and documents as tools for learning.

In addition, we need networks that facilitate the exchange of training materials through journals, seminars, and associations. Governments at all levels, companies of all sizes, and all types of educational institutions can assist this effort. Only in this way will we develop leaders and managers qualified to tackle the sustainable tourism challenges in the new millennium.

Several different approaches could be explored to increase sustainable tourism education and training. A starting point might be a world summit on sustainable tourism education sponsored by such organizations as the United Nations Development Program, the World Travel and Tourism Council, the World Tourism Organization, the Organization of American States, the Organisation for Economic Co-Operation and Development, APEC, the Caribbean Tourism Organization, the Earth Council, BEST, and the National Geographic Society. Other efforts might include local, national, and international seminar programs with specific sustainable tourism agendas. The future of sustainable tourism depends on the many organizations, educational institutions, businesses, governments, and not-for-profit entities sharing research, development, and education programs.

SUSTAINABLE TOURISM HAS ARRIVED AND IS HEALTHY

In conclusion, this book has built a case that tourism sustainability in essence means seeking economic growth and benefits in a way that preserves natural or built resources, provides a quality product to the visitor, and embraces local involvement. It strongly suggests that responsible tourism management must protect these resources while adding to an area's overall tourism product. Properly managed tourism offers a range of sustainable environmental benefits, including improved public facilities, protected rural areas, clean and attractive recreational opportunities, and the maintenance of important heritage, historical, and cultural venues and values. Importantly, it provides for an enhanced experience for visitors and adds to the quality of life of local citizens.

Environmentally responsible tourism development is emerging as a powerful instrument for the management of economic resources in communities. As a result, pristine natural areas, unique built environments, and cultural and heritage activities are growing in value. The mandate is to find the means to protect our natural and cultural heritage and make it accessible to large numbers of visitors. Sustainable tourism development will need to be better managed if travel is to respond to new consumer interests and desires in this millennium. The Maho Bay Campground on St. John in the U.S. Virgin Islands, the case study at the end of this chapter, exemplifies a very positive approach to sustainable tourism.

This book suggests that wonderful opportunities exist if sustainable tourism is approached in the right way. Well-planned and well-managed sustainable tourism can provide benefits at all economic levels, increase standards of living for local residents, and maintain or even improve the quality of the local environment. This does not mean that the tourism industry faces no problems now and in the future in its efforts toward tourism sustainability. Unfortunately, pollution, congestion, and degradation of the natural and built environment are found in almost every nation of the world. However, environmentally sustainable tourism practices can help to prevent or rectify undesirable outcomes, supporting economic gains from tourism development and tourist activities while preserving environmental, historic, and cultural resources that residents and tourists can continue to enjoy.[1]

In the popular book *Tourism: Principles, Practices, and Philosophies*, authors Charles R. Goeldner and J. R. Brent Ritchie (2006) succinctly explain the essence of why sustainable tourism development needs to be well planned and managed.

> Sustainable tourism development is development that has been carefully planned and managed. It is the antithesis of tourism that has developed for short-term gains. Because of the expected continuing growth of tourism, sustainable development is the approach that will be needed. Because of the pressure on the world's resources, it is the only sensible approach. (p. 490)

It is appropriate to end this chapter and the book with the case study on Maho Bay in the U.S. Virgin Islands, which was developed by Stanley Selengut, a civil engineer who also emerged as an ecotourism pioneer and eco-entrepreneur. Selengut's property has won more ecotourism awards than any other resort development in the world. *Islands Magazine* gave Maho Bay its Ecotourism Award for "pioneering the concept of a low-impact, ecologically sensitive resort in a protected environment, and for serving as a worldwide advocate and model for such projects" ("The Eco-Achievers" 1992). *In Business* magazine said that "[e]co-entrepreneur Stanley Selengut knows how to build sustainable quality into the planet's special places" and that for "Stanley Selengut, the best entertainment comes from designing and operating resorts that can be genuinely enjoyed on many levels . . . for countless generations to come" (Goldstein 1999, pp. 1, 18). Many of the same principles Selengut incorporated into Maho Bay are included in his other resort properties Harmony and Concordia. He proved that sustainable tourism properties can be highly profitable, and he would be the first to say that sustainable tourism development is good not only for the community, but also as a business investment.

Managing Sustainable Tourism: A Legacy for the Future is an effort to inform and educate a broad spectrum of the population about the importance of preserving our natural and built environment. It is meant to engender cooperation locally, statewide, provincially, regionally, nationally, and internationally as a way of meeting tomorrow's challenge for quality tourism. The task is enormous and will require courage, education, sacrifice, cooperation, and strong commitments at every level of government, industry, and society. The rewards are also enormous in that each generation will pass on a strong legacy of tourism benefits to those who follow. My summary of the legacy of sustainable tourism is, "Responsibly managed tourism enhances and enriches natural, heritage, and cultural values and embraces the need to preserve them so that the community and visitor have a quality tourism experience now and in the future."

CASE STUDY: SUSTAINABLE TOURISM IN THE U.S. VIRGIN ISLANDS, ST. JOHN— MAHO BAY, HARMONY, AND CONCORDIA

Over twenty-five years ago, Stanley Selengut opened the Maho Bay Campground on St. John in the U.S. Virgin Islands. His intention was to provide nature and camping enthusiasts the intimacy of the Caribbean outdoors, yet with more low-cost comfort and convenience than regular campgrounds. He combined his background as a civil engineer and carpenter with his love of the natural environment to create 114 tent-cottages linked by boardwalks to the camp office, general store in an open-air pavilion, bar, and cafeteria. The attractive raised walkways preserve the ground cover and increase the camp's carrying capacity with very little impact on the environment. Placing pipes and cables under the walkways eliminates the need to dig trenches. The washhouses contain low-flush toilets, spring-loaded faucets, and pull-chain cold-water showers. The platform tent-cottages are wooden floored and framed, with translucent fabric walls and screen windows that breathe with the cooling trade winds and make good use of the natural light. Each sixteen by sixteen foot cottage has a bedroom with two beds, a living room with a sofa that folds out to become a third bed, a cooking and dining area, and an open sundeck with a spectacular view overlooking Maho Bay. Bed linens, blankets, towels, and cooking and eating utensils are provided. Every cottage has an electric fan. The outdoor restaurant serves a varied and healthful breakfast and dinner every day. Next to the camp office is the activities desk, where campers can get information and sign up for activities such as sailing, scuba, night snorkeling, park events, fishing, windsurfing, kayaking, tours, and massage. No radios are allowed. Departing guests leave books and any unused supplies at the free help-yourself center for the benefit of incoming guests. A sense of peace and cooperation and community pervade the atmosphere. In the high season, the campground maintains a 95 percent occupancy rate.

Over the years, Stanley Selengut has striven to use human intervention to improve rather than degrade the natural environment. Measures have included feral animal control, removal of invasive vegetation, promotion of indigenous plants, and reintroduction of iguanas (long extinct on this part of the island) to control mosquitoes and other bugs. The result is that the fourteen acres of the campground are greener than the surrounding parklands, which are protected but receive no special attention to promote floral growth.

Inspired by a U.S. National Park Service book on sustainable design and new "green" technologies (Hart 1994), Selengut has two additional developments that provide an educational experience combining a natural setting with the comfort of a Caribbean hotel vacation based on sustainable development principles. The first site, Harmony, sits above the campground and contains twelve condominium units linked by raised walkways. These units are limited to two stories to reduce their visual pollution of the view from the bay; they are entirely solar powered and are constructed from recycled products and materials (such as compressed sawdust handrails and walkways, and nonstructural walls that are a mixture of waste cardboard and cement). Trees are pruned away from the photovoltaic cells on the roofs, where hot water is heated. Solar power is turned on with a key that also locks the front door, so guests must turn off the power whenever they leave their unit. Visitors can monitor their energy use on computers and so enjoyably learn new ways in which to live with low energy use, disconnected from utility companies. During the learning process, they become naturally energy conscious, and can then take this awareness with them when they return home.

Harmony's even more comfortable sister development, Concordia, is built on similar principles on the other side of the island. It has a hillside swimming pool (built with minimal site damage and no heavy equipment), laundry room, honor store, and more personal attention from onsite management.

Smithsonian Magazine and the American Society of Travel Agents (ASTA) awarded Maho Bay Camps Inc. its 1997 Environmental Award. The award, the highest in the travel industry, was presented on September 7 in Glasgow, Scotland. Maho Bay Campground, Harmony Resort, Estate Concordia Studios, and Concordia Eco-tents were all recognized as "prototype[s] for sustainable development, creating worldwide awareness of the benefits of ecotourism and the importance of protecting and preserving our environment." The ASTA/Smithsonian award is presented annually at ASTA's World Congress to two organizations that have made a significant contribution to the preservation of the environment.

As Selengut states in his literature, "If my experience has taught me anything, it is that we are not separate from nature, but an intimate part of it, and with that intimacy comes a profound responsibility that we accept, gratefully" (Inter-American Travel Congresses 1997).

Notes

Preface

1. Some studies refer to outdoor-based tourism as "ecotourism," whereas others use the term "nature-based tourism." These two terms are not technically synonymous: the term "ecotourism" suggests activities that promote conservation of nature, whereas "nature-based tourism" refers to broader activities such as fishing, hunting, camping, outdoor forest trails, and sometimes the use of recreational vehicles. However, they are often used in tourism for similar purposes, and, unless otherwise indicated, I will use them interchangeably.

2. "Coopetition" is a new term circulating throughout tourism circles in America. It has been included in the *Barnhart Dictionary Companion* and, as it gets used more often, will likely make it into the big-league dictionaries.

Chapter 1

1. For a fuller explanation of tourism policy development, including concerns for the environment, see Edgell (1990).

2. Although, technically, the words "travel" and "tourism" have different definitions, they are frequently used interchangeably, as they are in this book.

3. Bramwell et al. (1996) offer an enlightening discussion of some of the principles of sustainable tourism management in Europe. Although the book consists mainly of a series of case studies from different European countries, it does examine some of the potential benefits and pitfalls of implementing sustainable tourism management.

4. The World Tourism Organization (WTO), headquartered in Madrid, Spain, has been producing worldwide tourism statistics for more than twenty-five years. It also produces numerous tourism studies and is the best source for international tourism definitions and statistical standards.

5. For more information on this survey and related documents, contact the Travel Industry Association of America, Washington, DC.

6. This tripartite approach to sustainable tourism is discussed further in Chapter 10. The agenda document seeks to establish a policy and operational framework for the public and private sectors to achieve sustainable development. The World Travel and Tourism Council is composed of executives from major travel-related companies throughout the world.

7. Many of the areas and countries cited are taken from Tourtellot (2004); they were rated by a global panel of more than 200 experts.

8. For additional details, see Travel Industry Association of America (2003a,b: 14-15).

9. Jorgensen (1997) provides an excellent discussion of sustainable tourism development of Salt River in a detailed thirty-page study prepared for the Department of Social Anthropology, Aarhus University, Denmark. On site in St. Croix, Jorgensen conducted research and interviews to pull together important information into a very readable document.

10. William F. Cissel of the National Park Service, U.S. Virgin Islands, has prepared some excellent documents about St. Croix. See Cissel (1993a,b); also Vauthrin (1993).

11. One of the very best sources of information on the Salt River Bay National Historical Park and Ecological Preserve is Jessie K. Thomson, resident of St. Croix, who in 1993 served as President of the Christopher Columbus Jubilee Committee. She was part of the movement behind the establishment of the park and is dedicated to the dream of educating people about its significance as a key to "sustainability."

Chapter 2

1. See New Zealand Ministry of Tourism (1992), which presents excellent background materials summarizing tourism development within the concept of sustainability.

2. This section relies heavily on the concepts of sustainable tourism developed in Griffin and Boele's article.

3. For a discussion of some of the key policy issues, see the *Journal of Sustainable Tourism,* which began publication in 1993.

Chapter 3

1. BEST has done as much as any organization to bring together many of the key players in sustainable tourism development (see www.conferenceboard.org/best.htm).

2. It should be noted that many efforts toward sustainable tourism are being made in the Caribbean region. The Caribbean Tourism Organization has a small unit devoted to sustainable tourism issues and policies. However, a Caribbean-wide strategic tourism plan devoted solely to sustainable tourism is required so that each member state has something to draw on for technical help and direction.

Chapter 4

1. In the past, the World Tourism Organization was affiliated to the United Nations and advocated a strong voice for the UN in sustainable tourism. In December 2004, the it became an official part of the UN system. It remains to be seen how this organizational change will impact the policies and programs of the World Tourism Organization.

2. The Commission for Environmental Cooperation is a fairly new key player in sustainable tourism terms. Its efforts thus far demonstrate a pretty clear understanding of what needs to be accomplished by Canada, Mexico, and the United States. If

the organization is successful it could provide the model for other multinational organizations.

3. The case study is based on an unpublished technical report by Gerald P. Bauer and Jerry Wylie of the U.S. Department of Agriculture Forest Service, International Institute of Tropical Forestry (Wylie and Bauer 2002).

Chapter 5

1. Many books provide accounts of cultural tourism, but none offers a more thorough presentation than McKercher and du Cross (2002).

Chapter 6

1. The National Trust for Historic Preservation produces excellent materials on heritage tourism. Anyone researching or specializing in heritage and cultural tourism in the United States should access as much of the trust's information as possible. Contact National Trust for Historic Preservation, 1785 Massachusetts Avenue, NW; Washington, DC, 20036/(202)588-6000.

Chapter 7

1. This chapter draws heavily on concepts developed in Edgell (2002).

Chapter 8

1. Boo (1990) also provides a good discussion of ecotourism.

2. This brochure is available from Tallgrass Prairie National Preserve, Rt. 1 Box 14; Strong City, KS, 66869.

Chapter 9

1. See the papers from the "Globe '90 Conference," in Vancouver, BC, Canada (Globe '90, Tourism Stream Action Strategy Committee 1990). Many of the ideas and commentary in this section have their origins in this conference.

Chapter 10

1. The Asia-Pacific Economic Cooperation Secretariat (1996) provides an excellent overview of sustainable tourism, based on a study of the APEC countries conducted by Apogee Research, Inc. Although the focus is on the APEC countries, much of the information is useful reading for the general principles and applications of sustainable tourism.

Bibliography

Acott, T.G., LaTrobe, H.L., and Howard, S.H. (1998). "An Evaluation of Deep Eco-tourism and Shallow Tourism." *Journal of Sustainable Tourism* 6(3).

Allen, William and Carlton, John G. (2000). "Cahokia Mounds: Saving the Past." *St. Louis Post-Dispatch,* January 9, pp. A6-7.

Andrews, Edmund L. (2003). "Iraqi Looters Tearing up Archaeological Sites." *The New York Times,* May 23, pp. A1,13.

Archer, Brian (1996). "Sustainable Tourism—Do Economists Really Care?" *Progress in Tourism and Hospitality Research* 2(3/4, September/December): 217-222.

Ash, John and Turner, Louis (1976). *The Golden Hordes: International Tourism and the Pleasure Periphery.* New York: St. Martin's Press.

Asia-Pacific Economic Cooperation Secretariat (1996). "Environmentally Sustainable Tourism in APEC Member Economies." Singapore: APEC.

Banff National Park (1996). "Banff—Bow Valley: At the Crossroads" Summary Report. Available from Superintendent, Banff National Park, Box 900, Banff, Alberta, Canada, October.

Beebe, William (1924). *Galápagos: World's End.* New York: Dover Publications.

Belland, Greg and Zinkin, Charlie (1995). "Heritage Tourism in Canada's Rocky Mountain Parks: A Case Study in Education and Partnership." In Neil W.P. Munro and J.H. Martin Willisson (eds.), *Linking Protected Areas with Working Landscapes Conserving Biodiversity: Proceedings of the Third International Conference on Science and Management of Protected Areas, 12-16 May 1997* (pp. 616-625). Wolfville, Nova Scotia, Canada: Science and Management of Protected Areas Association.

Biondi, Joann (1996). "Of Manors & Mansions." *Caribbean Travel and Life,* June, pp. 82-91.

Boers, H. and Bosch, M. (1994). *The Earth As a Holiday Resort.* Utrecht, the Netherlands: Institute for Environmental Communications and Netherlands Institute of Transport and Tourism Studies.

Boo, Elizabeth (1990). *Ecotourism: The Potentials and Pitfalls,* 2 vols. Washington, DC: World Wide Fund for Nature.

Braithwaite, Richard (1993). "Ecotourism in the Monsoonal Tropics." *Issues 23* (May): 29-36.

Bramwell, Bill, Henry, Ian, Jackson, Guy, Goytia Prat, Ana, Richards, Greg, and der Straaten, Janvan (1996). *Sustainable Tourism Management: Principles and Practice.* The Netherlands: Tilburg University Press.

Bramwell, Bill and Lane, Bernard (1993-1997). *Journal of Sustainable Tourism.* Avon, United Kingdom: Channel View Publications.

Brandenburger, Adam M. and Nalebuff, Barry J. (1996). *Co-opetition.* New York: Doubleday.

Brass, Jane L. (Ed.) (1994). *Community Tourism Assessment Handbook.* Corvallis, OR: Western Rural Development Center, Oregon State University.

Burr, Steven W. (1995). "What Research Says about Sustainable Tourism Development." *Parks and Recreation 30*(9, September). Available online at www.find articles.com/p/articles/mi_m1145/is_n9_v30/ai_17498055.

Business Enterprises for Sustainable Travel (n.d.). "Lindblad Expeditions: Tour Operator Taps into Travelers' Philanthropic Impulses." New York: BEST.

Butler, R. and J. Jenkins (Eds.) (1998). *Tourism and Recreation in Rural Areas.* Chichester, UK: John Wiley and Sons.

Center for Sustainable Tourism (2000). "A Guide to New Technology for Rural Tourism Operators." Boulder: Colorado University of Colorado at Boulder.

"Ceremony Dedicates Preserve as a Park" (1997). *The Topeka Capital Journal,* June 1, pp. 1A-2A.

Chapman, Matthew (2003). "Islands of the Fittest." *National Geographic Traveler,* April, pp. 45-57.

Cissel, William F. (1993a). "A Summary of the Natural and Cultural Resource Significance of Salt River Bay National Historical Park and Ecological Preserve." St. Croix, U.S. Virgin Islands: U.S. National Park Service, September.

Cissel, William F. (1993b). "A Synopis of the Archaeological and Historical Significance of Salt River, St. Croix, U.S. Virgin Islands, with Its Special Relevance to the Columbus Quincentennial." February. St. Croix, U.S. Virgin Islands: National Park Service.

Coccossis, Harry and Nijkamp, Peter (1995). *Sustainable Tourism Development.* Brookfield, VT: Ashgate.

Commission for Environmental Cooperation (1999). "Sustainable Tourism in Natural Areas (99-01-05)," "The Development of Sustainable Tourism in Natural Areas." Discussion paper prepared for "A Dialogue on Sustainable Tourism in Natural Areas in North America," May 27-28, Playa del Carmen, Mexico.

Commission for Environmental Cooperation (2000). "Promoting Sustainable Tourism in North America's Natural Areas: The Steps Forward." Note by Secretariat for Environmental Cooperation, Montreal, May.

Darwin, Charles (1997). *The Voyage of the Beagle.* 2003-2005 Project Gutenberg Literary Archive Foundation.

Darwin, Charles (1999). *The Origin of Species by Means of Natural Selection,* Sixth Edition. 2003-2005 Project Gutenberg Literary Archive Foundation.

deKadt, Emanuel (1990). "Making the Alternative Sustainable: Lessons from Development for Tourism." Discussion Paper No. 272. Brighton, United Kingdom: Institute for Development Studies at the University of Sussex.

Department of Canadian Heritage (1997). "Parks Canada's Response to the Bow Valley Study." January 24. Available from Parks Canada, Superintendent, Banff National Park, Box 900, Banff, Alberta Canada.

Duncan, Barbara C. and Riggs, Brett H. (2003). *Cherokee Heritage Trails Guidebook.* Chapel Hill and London: The University of North Carolina Press.

Eagles, P.F.J. and Cascagnette, J.W. (1995). "Canadian Ecotourists: Who Are They?" *Tourism Recreation Research 20:* 22-28.

"The Eco-Achievers" (1992). *Islands Magazine,* September/October.

Ecotourism Society (1994). "Ecotourism Guidelines for Nature Tour Operators." Bennington, VT: Ecotourism Society.

Edgell, David L., Sr. (1990). *International Tourism Policy.* New York: Van Nostrand Reinhold.

Edgell, David L., Sr. (1993). *World Tourism at the Millennium.* Washington, DC: U.S. Department of Commerce.

Edgell, David L., Sr. (1997a). "Managing Sustainable Tourism in the Next Millennium." Speech at the International Education Seminar, June 16-19, Anchorage, Alaska.

Edgell, David L., Sr. (1997b). "Sustaining Tourism by Managing Its Natural and Heritage Resource." Paper presented at the XVII Inter-American Travel Congress, April 7-11, San Jose, Costa Rica.

Edgell, David L., Sr. (1999). *Tourism Policy: The Next Millennium.* Champaign, IL: Sagamore Publishing.

Edgell, David L., Sr. (2002). *Best Practices Guidebook for International Tourism Development for Rural Communities.* Provo, UT: Brigham Young University.

Edgell, David L., Sr. (2005). "Sustainable Tourism as an Economic Development Strategy in the Waterways and Coastlines of North Carolina." East Carolina University, Institute for Tourism, September.

Edgell, David L., Sr. and Cartwright, Mary Lynn (1990). "How One Kansas Town Used Tourism to Revitalize Its Economic Base." *Business America,* November 5, pp. 14-17.

Edgell, David L., Sr. and Dalton, Sarah J. (1993). "Home on the Road: Exploring Rural America Is a Commanding Business Asset." *Business America,* November 29, pp. 18-20.

Edgell, David L., Sr. and Haenisch, R. Todd (1995). *Competition: Global Tourism beyond the Millennium.* Kansas City, MO: International Policy Publishing.

Edgell, David L., Sr. and Harbaugh, Linda (1993). "Tourism Development: An Economic Stimulus in the Heart of America." *Business America,* January 25, pp. 16-17.

Edgell, David L., Sr., Hayden, Gin, and DiPersio, Cindy (1998). *Sustainable Tourism Information Source.* Boulder: Center for Sustainable Tourism, College of Business and Administration, University of Colorado at Boulder, February.

Edgell, David L., Sr. and Hayes, Bernetta J. (1998). "Cultural Richness in the U.S. Black Community Offers Great Potential for Tourism Development." *Business America,* September 26, pp. 8-9.

Edgell, David L., Sr. and Smith, Ginger (2000). "Environmental and Cultural Sustainability: Tourism Promotion in the New Millennium." Paper presented at the International Conference 2000: Cultural Tourism in the New Millennium, October 17-18, Kwangu City, Korea.

Edgell, David L., Sr. and Staiger, Lee (1992). "A Small Community Adopts Tourism as a Development Tool." *Business America,* April 20, pp. 16-20.

Evaluación de la Cuenca Hidrográfica del Canal de Panama (1995). Panama City, Panama: Editora Sibauste, ANCON.

"Fair Trade: Ranchers Bank on Conservation" (2004). *Nature Conservancy 54*(1, Spring): 20-21. Arlington, VA.

Fogarty, David and Renkow, Mitch (1998). "Agritourism Opportunities for North Carolina." *Resource Economics and Policy* (AREP97-2). Available online at www.bae.ncsu.edu/bae/programs/extension/publicat/arep/arep2.htm.

Fussell, Fred C. (2003). *Blue Ridge Music Trails: Finding a Place in the Circle.* Chapel Hill and London: The University of North Carolina Press.

Garfield, Donald (Ed.) (1997). *Partners in Tourism: Culture and Commerce.* Washington, DC: American Association of Museums.

Garrod, Brian and Fyall, Alan (1998). "Beyond the Rhetoric of Sustainable Tourism?" *Tourism Management 19*(3): 199-212.

Gartner, William C. (1996). *Tourism Development: Principles, Processes, and Policies.* New York: Van Nostrand Reinhold.

Globe '90, Tourism Stream Action Strategy Committee (1990). *An Action Strategy for Sustainable Tourism Development.* Tourism Canada, March.

Goeldner, Charles R. and Ritchie, J.R. Brent (2003). *Tourism: Principles, Practices, Philosophies,* Ninth Edition. New York: John Wiley and Sons

Goeldner, Charles R. and Ritchie, J.R. Brent (2006). *Tourism: Principles, Practices, Philosophies,* Tenth Edition. Hoboken, NJ: John Wiley and Sons.

Goeldner, Charles R., Ritchie, J.R. Brent and McIntosh, Robert W. (2000). *Tourism: Principles, Practices, Philosophies.* New York: John Wiley and Sons.

Goldstein, Jerome (1999). "The Logical Path of an Ecotourism Pioneer." *In Business,* July/August, pp.18-19.

"Great Smoky Mountains National Park" (2004). *North Carolina Outdoor Recreation Guide,* 8-11. Morganton, NC: Granite Communications.

Green Globe (1994). *Environmental Management for Your Business: An Introductory Guide.* London: Green Globe.

Griffin, Tony, and Boele, Nicolette (1993). "Alternative Paths to Sustainable Tourism." *The Annual Review of Travel.* New York: American Express Travel Related Services.

Harris, Rob, Griffin, Tony, and Williams, Peter (2002). *Sustainable Tourism: A Global Perspective.* Burlington, MA: Butterworth-Heineman.

Hart, Leslie Starr (1994). *Guiding Principles of Sustainable Design.* Denver, CO: National Parks Service, Denver Service Center. Available online at www.nps.gov/dsc/d_publications/d_1_gpsd.htm.

Hawkes, Susanne and Williams, Peter (Eds.) (1993). *The Greening of Tourism from Principles to Practice.* Burnaby, BC: Simon Fraser University, March.

Hawkins, Donald E. and Ritchie, J.R. Brent (Eds.) (1991). *World Travel and Tourism Review.* Wallingford, United Kingdom: C.A.B. International.

Hawley, Peter (1991). "Historic Preservation and Tourism." In *Enhancing Rural Economies through Amenity Resources* (pp. 22-30). College Park: Pennsylvania State University.

Heat-Moon, William L. (1991). *PrairyErth.* Boston: Houghton Mifflin Company.

"Highlights of Minister's Direction for the Banff Bow Valley and Response to the Bow Valley Study Report" (1997). Department of Canadian Heritage. Available from Superintendent, Banff National Park, Box 900, Banff, Alberta, Canada.

Hiller, Herbert L. (1996). "Marketing Florida." *Florida Trend,* March, pp. 41-49.

Holland, Adam C. (1998). "Public Has Its Say on Preserve." *Kansas City Star,* June 9, pp. B1, 4.

Illinois Historic Preservation Agency (1997). "Cahokia Mounds State Historic Site Brochure." Collinsville, IL: Illinois Historic Preservation Agency.

Inskeep, Edward (1991). *Tourism Planning: An Integrated and Sustainable Development Approach.* New York: Van Nostrand Reinhold.

Inter-American Travel Congresses (1997). "Sustaining Tourism by Managing Its Natural and Heritage Resources." Available online at http://www.oas.org/TOURISM/docnet/Iatc3en.htm.

Jorgensen, Janne (1997). "Case Study: Salt River, St. Croix." Aarhus, Denmark: Aarhus University, February.

Koth, Barbara, Kreag, Glenn, and Sem, John (1991). *Rural Tourism Development.* St. Paul: University of Minnesota.

Lancaster County Planning Commission (1998). "Heritage Tourism Plan." Lancaster, PA: Lancaster County Planning Commission, January.

Lane, Bernard (1997). "Marketing for Sustainable Agri-tourism: The Strategic Importance of Sustainability." Address presented in Reykjavik, Iceland, September.

Lawson, John (1709/1967). *A New Voyage to Carolina* [abbreviated title], ed. Talmage Lefler, Hugh. Chapel Hill: The University of North Carolina Press.

Lindberg, Kreg (1991). *Policies for Maximizing Nature Tourism's Ecological and Economic Benefits.* Washington, DC: World Resources Institute.

Liu, Juanita C. (1994). *Pacific Islands Ecotourism: A Public Policy and Planning Guide.* Honolulu, HI: Pacific Business Center, University of Hawaii at Manoa.

Lord, Lewis (1999). "The Americas." *U.S. News and World Report,* August 16. Available online at www.usnews.com/usnews/culture/articles/990816/Archive_001717_3.htm.

Lynch, Ida P. (2003). "Paddle the Mighty Roanoke." *Wildlife in North Carolina,* April, p. 2.

Magruder, I. Katherine (2000). "Assessment and Strategic Plan for Tourism Development in Caroline County, Maryland." Queenstown, MD, January.

Magruder, I. Katherine (2002). "Natural Advantage (An Initiative to Develop Ecotourism in Queen Anne's County)." Chester, MD: Queen Anne's County, Department of Business and Tourism, March.

Malley, Michael (1999). "Turning Green Practices into Greenbacks." *Hotels and Hotel Management,* May 17.

May, Vincent (1991). "Tourism, Environment and Development—Values, Sustainability and Stewardship." *Tourism Management 12*(2, June): 112-118.

McIntyre, G. and Hetherington, A. (1992). *Sustainable Tourism Development: Guidelines for Local Planners.* Bainbridge Island, WA: Meta-Link, Inc.

McKercher, Bob and du Cros, Hilary (2002). *Cultural Tourism: The Partnership Between Tourism and Cultural Heritage Management.* Binghamton, NY: The Haworth Hospitality Press.

Minister of Public Works and Government Services Canada (1997). "Banff National Park Management Plan Summary." April. Available from Superintendent, Banff National Park, Box 900, Alberta, Canada.

Moskin, Bill and Guettler, Sandy (1998). "State of Missouri Cultural Tourism Development Plan." Bainbridge Island, WA. Plans submitted June 15, 1998.

Motavalli, Jim (2002). "Taking the Natural Path." *The Environmental Magazine 13*(4, July/August): 26-36.

Naisbitt, John (1994). *Global Paradox.* New York: William Morrow and Company, Inc.

National Geographic Traveler and Travel Industry Association of America (2002). *The Geotourism Study: Phase I Executive Summary.* Washington, DC: Travel Industry Association of America.

National Park Service (1991). "Special Resource Study on the Z-Bar (Spring Hill) Ranch." Washington, DC: National Park Service, March.

National Park Service (2005). "Our Mission." Available online at www.nps.gov/legacy/mission.html.

National Park System Advisory Board Report (2001). *Rethinking the National Parks for the 21st Century.* Wilmington, MA: National Geographic Society, July.

National Park Trust (1994). "National Park Trust Acquires Historic Tallgrass Prairie Ranch." Washington, DC: National Park Trust, June 3.

National Park Trust (1996). "America's Prairie Heritage: Creating a Tallgrass Park." Washington, DC: National Park Trust.

National Trust for Historic Preservation (1998). "Authentic Heritage Tourism." *Forum News,* March/April. Washington, DC.

National Trust for Historic Preservation (1999). "Getting Started: How to Succeed in Heritage Tourism." Washington, DC: National Trust for Historic Preservation.

National Trust for Historic Preservation (2001a). "Share Your Heritage: Cultural Heritage Tourism Success Stories." Washington, DC: National Trust for Historic Preservation.

National Trust for Historic Preservation (2001b). "Share Your Heritage: Cultural and Heritage Tourism—The Same or Different?" Washington, DC: National Trust for Historic Preservation.

National Trust for Historic Preservation (2001c). *Stories Across America: Opportunities for Rural Tourism.* Washington, DC: National Trust for Historic Preservation.

Nelson, J.G., Butler, R., and Wall, G. (Eds.) (1993). *Tourism and Sustainable Development: Monitoring, Planning, Managing.* Joint Publication Number 1. Ontario, Canada: Heritage Resource Centre, University of Waterloo.

New Zealand Ministry of Tourism (1992). "Tourism Sustainability: A Discussion Paper." Issues Paper No. 2. Wellington, New Zealand: New Zealand Ministry of Tourism, December.

Organisation for Economic Co-Operation and Development (1994). "Tourism Policy and International Tourism in OECD Countries 1991-1992." Paris: OECD.

Organisation of East Caribbean States (n.d.). "Improving Waste Management and Port Waste Reception in the Caribbean." Available online at www.oceanatlas.com/unatlas/uses/uneptextsph/wastesph/2596carib.html.

Organization of American States (1995). "Sustainable Nature and Heritage Tourism Development: A Summary of OAS Technical Assistance in the Caribbean." Washington, DC: OAS.

Pigram, John J. (1990). "Sustainable Tourism Policy Considerations." *The Journal of Tourism Studies 1*(2, November).

Porter, Michael (2004). *Competitiveness in Rural U.S. Regions: Learning and Research Agenda.* Harvard Business School Report, February 25.

Priestley, G.K., Edwards, J.A., and Coccossis, H. (Eds.) (1996). *Sustainable Tourism: European Experiences.* New York: Oxford University Press.

Public Law 102-372. "Tourism Policy and Export Promotion Act of 1992." September 30, 1992.

Ritchie, J.R. Brent and Goeldner, Charles R. (Eds.) (1994). *Travel, Tourism, and Hospitality Research.* New York: John Wiley and Sons.

Rubin, Kenneth I. (1997). "Incentives and Enforcement for Resource Management: Toward Environmentally Sustainable Tourism." Paper presented at the XVII Inter-American Travel Congress, April 7-11, San Jose, Costa Rica.

"Salt River Could Be World Heritage Site" (1993). Editorial, *The Daily News,* February 24. St. Thomas, U.S. Virgin Islands.

Selengut, Stanley (1992). "Resort Development in Partnership with Nature." Paper presented at the IVth World Congress on National Parks and Protected Areas, February 19-20, Caracas, Venezuela.

Sem, John, Teskey, Mike, and Watchorn, Liz (1997). "Experiences and Benefits: A Heritage Tourism Development Model." Ogden, UT: U.S. Forest Service, July.

Smith, Ginger (2000). "Environmental and Cultural Sustainability Through Tourism Promotion." International Conference: Cultural Tourism in the New Millennium, October 18, Kwangju City, Republic of Korea.

Stabler, M.J. (Ed.) (1997). *Tourism and Sustainability: Principles to Practice.* New York: Oxford University Press.

Tourtellot, Jonathan B. (2004). "Destination Scorecard, 115 Places Rated." *National Geographic Traveler 21*(2, March): 60-67.

Tourtellot, Jonathan B. (2005). "Destination Scorecard: How Do 55 National Park Regions Rate?" *National Geographic Traveler 22*(5, July/August): 80-92.

Travel Industry Association of America (n.d.). "Domestic Travel Fast Facts: Travel Trends from A to Z." Available online at www.tia.org/pressmedia/domestic_a_to_z.html.

Travel Industry Association of America (2002). *Tourism Works for America,* Eleventh Annual Edition. Washington, DC: TIA.

Travel Industry Association of America (2003a). *Geotourism: The New Trend in Travels.* Commissioned by *National Geographic Traveler.* Washington, DC: TIA.

Travel Industry Association of America (2003b). *Tourism Works for America,* Twelfth Annual Edition. Washington, DC: TIA.

Travel Industry Association of America (2004). *Tourism Works for America,* Thirteenth Annual Edition. Washington, DC: TIA.

Travel Industry Association of America, Research Department (2002). "The Geotourism Study: Phase I Executive Summary." Washington, DC: TIA.

Travels of Marco Polo (1958). Translated with an introduction by Ronald Latham. New York: Penguin Books Ltd.

U.S. Consulate General in Barcelona, Spain (2003). "Sustainable Tourism's Annotated Web Sites." Barcelona, Spain.

U.S. Department of Agriculture, Forest Service (1997). Report: "Experience and Benefits: A Heritage Tourism Development Model." Ogden, UT, July.

Vauthrin, Carla D. (1993). *Legacy to Treasure.* St. Croix, U.S. Virgin Islands: Clipper Press.

"Visit America's Newest National Park." (1996/7). *A Visitor's Guide to Chase County,* Fall/Winter, p. 1.

Weaver, Glenn D. (1993). *Tourism Development: A Guideline for Rural Communities.* Columbia: University of Missouri.

Welch, Ron (1995). "Prairie Preserved." *Kansas 3:* 2-5.

"Welcome to the Tallgrass Prairie National Preserve" (1997). *A Visitor's Guide to Chase County,* Spring/Summer. Tallgrass Prairie National Preserve. Route 1, Box 14, Strong, KS 66869.

Wiens, Janet (1999). "Green Meets High-tech: Hotel Conveys Environmental Nature Through Materials and Visual Impact." *ISdesigNET Magazine* (April). Available online at www.isdesignet.com/Magazine/April'99/green.html.

Wilder, Laura Ingalls (1935/2004). *Little House on the Prairie.* New York: HarperCollins.

World Tourism Organization (1992). *Guidelines: Development of National Parks and Protected Areas for Tourism.* Madrid, Spain: World Tourism Organization.

World Tourism Organization (1993). *Sustainable Tourism Development: Guide for Local Planners*. Madrid, Spain: World Tourism Organization.

World Tourism Organization (1995a). *Handbook on Natural Disaster Reduction in Tourist Areas*. Madrid, Spain: World Tourism Organization.

World Tourism Organization (1995b). *National and Regional Tourism Planning: Methodologies and Case Studies*. London: World Tourism Organization.

World Tourism Organization (1995c). *Tourism Market Trends—Americas*. Madrid, Spain: World Tourism Organization.

World Tourism Organization (2004). *Indicators of Sustainable Development for Tourism Destinations: A Guidebook*. Madrid, Spain: World Tourism Organization.

World Tourism Organization (2005). *WTO World Tourism Barometer* 3(2, June). Available online at www.world-tourism.org/newsroom/menu.htm.

World Travel and Tourism Council (n.d.). "Agenda 21 for the Travel & Tourism Industry: Towards Environmentally Sustainable Development." Available from WTTC, London, United Kingdom.

World Travel and Tourism Council, International Hotel and Restaurant Association, International Federation of Tour Operators, and the International Council of Cruise Lines (2002). "Industry as a Partner for Sustainable Development." United Nations Tourism Environment Program. London: WTTC.

World Travel and Tourism Council, World Tourism Organization and Earth Council (1995). *Agenda 21 for the Travel and Tourism Industry: Toward Environmentally Sustainable Development*. London, United Kingdom: WTTC.

Wylie, Jerry and Bauer, Jerry (2002). "Cultural and Nature Tourism at the Emberá Drua Community, Upper Chagres River." Unpublished Technical Report submitted to USAID/Panama. Rio Piedras, Puerto Rico: U.S. Forest Service, International Institute of Tropical Forestry.

Zeigler, Joanne F. (ed.) (1991). Enhancing Rural Economies Through Amenity Resources: A National Policy Symposium. State College: Pennsylvania State University.

Internet Resources

(Accessed May 30, 2005.)
http://www.geo.cornell.edu/geology/GalapagosWWW/Colonization.html
http://www.geo.cornell.edu/geology/GalapagosWWW/Darwin.html
http://www.geo.cornell.edu/geology/GalapagosWWW/Discovery.html
http://www.roanokeriverpartners.org

Index

THE HAWORTH HOSPITALITY PRESS®
Hospitality, Travel, and Tourism
K. S. Chon, PhD, Editor in Chief

THE TOURISM AND LEISURE INDUSTRY: SHAPING THE FUTURE edited by Klaus Weiermair and Christine Mathies. (2004). "If you need or want to know about the impact of globalization, the impact of technology, societal forces of change, the experience economy, adaptive technologies, environmental changes, or the new trend of slow tourism, you need this book. *The Tourism and Leisure Industry* contains a great mix of research and practical information." *Charles R. Goeldner, PhD, Professor Emeritus of Marketing and Tourism, Leeds School of Business, University of Colorado*

OCEAN TRAVEL AND CRUISING: A CULTURAL ANALYSIS by Arthur Asa Berger. (2004). "Dr. Berger presents an interdisciplinary discussion of the cruise industry for the thinking person. This is an enjoyable social psychology travel guide with a little business management thrown in. A great book for the curious to read a week before embarking on a first cruise or for the frequent cruiser to gain a broader insight into exactly what a cruise experience represents." *Carl Braunlich, DBA, Associate Professor, Department of Hospitality and Tourism Management, Purdue University, West Lafayette, Indiana*

STANDING THE HEAT: ENSURING CURRICULUM QUALITY IN CULINARY ARTS AND GASTRONOMY by Joseph A. Hegarty. (2003). "This text provides the genesis of a well-researched, thoughtful, rigorous, and sound theoretical framework for the enlargement and expansion of higher education programs in culinary arts and gastronomy." *John M. Antun, PhD, Founding Director, National Restaurant Institute, School of Hotel, Restaurant, and Tourism Management, University of South Carolina*

SEX AND TOURISM: JOURNEYS OF ROMANCE, LOVE, AND LUST edited by Thomas G. Bauer and Bob McKercher. (2003). "Anyone interested in or concerned about the impact of tourism on society and particularly in the developing world, should read this book. It explores a subject that has long remained ignored, almost a taboo area for many governments, institutions, and organizations. It demonstrates that the stereotyping of 'sex tourism' is too simple and travel and sex have many manifestations. The book follows its theme in an innovative and original way." *Carson L. Jenkins, PhD, Professor of International Tourism, University of Strathclyde, Glasgow, Scotland*

CONVENTION TOURISM: INTERNATIONAL RESEARCH AND INDUSTRY PERSPECTIVES edited by Karin Weber and Kye-Sung Chon. (2002). "This comprehensive book is truly global in its perspective. The text points out areas of needed research—a great starting point for graduate students, university faculty, and industry professionals alike. While the focus is mainly academic, there is a lot of meat for this burgeoning industry to chew on as well." *Patti J. Shock, CPCE, Professor and Department Chair, Tourism and Convention Administration, Harrah College of Hotel Administration, University of Nevada–Las Vegas*

CULTURAL TOURISM: THE PARTNERSHIP BETWEEN TOURISM AND CULTURAL HERITAGE MANAGEMENT by Bob McKercher and Hilary du Cros. (2002). "The book brings together concepts, perspectives, and practicalities that must be understood by both cultural heritage and tourism managers, and as such is a must-read for both." *Hisashi B. Sugaya, AICP, Former Chair, International Council of Monuments and Sites, International Scientific Committee on Cultural Tourism; Former Executive Director, Pacific Asia Travel Association Foundation, San Francisco, CA*

TOURISM IN THE ANTARCTIC: OPPORTUNITIES, CONSTRAINTS, AND FUTURE PROSPECTS by Thomas G. Bauer. (2001). "Thomas Bauer presents a wealth of detailed information on the challenges and opportunities facing tourism operators in this last great tourism frontier." *David Mercer, PhD, Associate Professor, School of Geography & Environmental Science, Monash University, Melbourne, Australia*

SERVICE QUALITY MANAGEMENT IN HOSPITALITY, TOURISM, AND LEISURE edited by Jay Kandampully, Connie Mok, and Beverley Sparks. (2001). "A must-read. . . . a treasure. . . . pulls together the work of scholars across the globe, giving you access to new ideas, international research, and industry examples from around the world." *John Bowen, Professor and Director of Graduate Studies, William F. Harrah College of Hotel Administration, University of Nevada, Las Vegas*

TOURISM IN SOUTHEAST ASIA: A NEW DIRECTION edited by K. S. (Kaye) Chon. (2000). "Presents a wide array of very topical discussions on the specific challenges facing the tourism industry in Southeast Asia. A great resource for both scholars and practitioners." *Dr. Hubert B. Van Hoof, Assistant Dean/Associate Professor, School of Hotel and Restaurant Management, Northern Arizona University*

THE PRACTICE OF GRADUATE RESEARCH IN HOSPITALITY AND TOURISM edited by K. S. Chon. (1999). "An excellent reference source for students pursuing graduate degrees in hospitality and tourism." *Connie Mok, PhD, CHE, Associate Professor, Conrad N. Hilton College of Hotel and Restaurant Management, University of Houston, Texas*

THE INTERNATIONAL HOSPITALITY MANAGEMENT BUSINESS: MANAGEMENT AND OPERATIONS by Larry Yu. (1999). "The abundant real-world examples and cases provided in the text enable readers to understand the most up-to-date developments in international hospitality business." *Zheng Gu, PhD, Associate Professor, College of Hotel Administration, University of Nevada, Las Vegas*

CONSUMER BEHAVIOR IN TRAVEL AND TOURISM by Abraham Pizam and Yoel Mansfeld. (1999). "A must for anyone who wants to take advantage of new global opportunities in this growing industry." *Bonnie J. Knutson, PhD, School of Hospitality Business, Michigan State University*

LEGALIZED CASINO GAMING IN THE UNITED STATES: THE ECONOMIC AND SOCIAL IMPACT edited by Cathy H. C. Hsu. (1999). "Brings a fresh new look at one of the areas in tourism that has not yet received careful and serious consideration in the past." *Muzaffer Uysal, PhD, Professor of Tourism Research, Virginia Polytechnic Institute and State University, Blacksburg*

HOSPITALITY MANAGEMENT EDUCATION edited by Clayton W. Barrows and Robert H. Bosselman. (1999). "Takes the mystery out of how hospitality management education programs function and serves as an excellent resource for individuals interested in pursuing the field." *Joe Perdue, CCM, CHE, Director, Executive Masters Program, College of Hotel Administration, University of Nevada, Las Vegas*

MARKETING YOUR CITY, U.S.A.: A GUIDE TO DEVELOPING A STRATEGIC TOURISM MARKETING PLAN by Ronald A. Nykiel and Elizabeth Jascolt. (1998). "An excellent guide for anyone involved in the planning and marketing of cities and regions. . . . A terrific job of synthesizing an otherwise complex procedure." *James C. Maken, PhD, Associate Professor, Babcock Graduate School of Management, Wake Forest University, Winston-Salem, North Carolina*

Order a copy of this book with this form or online at:
http://www.haworthpress.com/store/product.asp?sku=5489

MANAGING SUSTAINABLE TOURISM
A Legacy for the Future

_____in hardbound at $39.95 (ISBN-13: 978-0-7890-2770-2; ISBN-10: 0-7890-2770-4)

_____in softbound at $19.95 (ISBN-13: 978-0-7890-2771-9; ISBN-10: 0-7890-2771-2)

Or order online and use special offer code HEC25 in the shopping cart.

COST OF BOOKS_____

POSTAGE & HANDLING_____
*(US: $4.00 for first book & $1.50
for each additional book)*
*(Outside US: $5.00 for first book
& $2.00 for each additional book)*

SUBTOTAL_____

IN CANADA: ADD 7% GST_____

STATE TAX_____
*(NJ, NY, OH, MN, CA, IL, IN, PA, & SD
residents, add appropriate local sales tax)*

FINAL TOTAL_____
*(If paying in Canadian funds,
convert using the current
exchange rate, UNESCO
coupons welcome)*

☐ **BILL ME LATER:** (Bill-me option is good on
US/Canada/Mexico orders only; not good to
jobbers, wholesalers, or subscription agencies.)
☐ Check here if billing address is different from
shipping address and attach purchase order and
billing address information.

Signature_____

☐ **PAYMENT ENCLOSED: $_____**

☐ **PLEASE CHARGE TO MY CREDIT CARD.**

☐ Visa ☐ MasterCard ☐ AmEx ☐ Discover
☐ Diner's Club ☐ Eurocard ☐ JCB

Account # _____

Exp. Date_____

Signature_____

Prices in US dollars and subject to change without notice.

NAME_____

INSTITUTION_____

ADDRESS_____

CITY_____

STATE/ZIP_____

COUNTRY_____ COUNTY (NY residents only)_____

TEL_____ FAX_____

E-MAIL_____

May we use your e-mail address for confirmations and other types of information? ☐ Yes ☐ No
We appreciate receiving your e-mail address and fax number. Haworth would like to e-mail or fax special
discount offers to you, as a preferred customer. **We will never share, rent, or exchange your e-mail address
or fax number.** We regard such actions as an invasion of your privacy.

Order From Your Local Bookstore or Directly From
The Haworth Press, Inc.
10 Alice Street, Binghamton, New York 13904-1580 • USA
TELEPHONE: 1-800-HAWORTH (1-800-429-6784) / Outside US/Canada: (607) 722-5857
FAX: 1-800-895-0582 / Outside US/Canada: (607) 771-0012
E-mail to: orders@haworthpress.com

For orders outside US and Canada, you may wish to order through your local
sales representative, distributor, or bookseller.
For information, see http://haworthpress.com/distributors

(Discounts are available for individual orders in US and Canada only, not booksellers/distributors.)
PLEASE PHOTOCOPY THIS FORM FOR YOUR PERSONAL USE.
http://www.HaworthPress.com   BOF04